Lindsey Campbell

Techniques and Projects to Take You Further

# Welcome to WEAVING 2

SCHIFFER
PUBLISHING

4880 Lower Valley Road • Atglen, PA 19310

hello hydrangea

Designed by Danielle D. Farmer
Cover design by Danielle D. Farmer
Type set in Silver South Script/Playfair Display/Merriweather/DIN-Light

ISBN: 978-0-7643-5768-8
Printed in China

Published by Schiffer Publishing, Ltd.
4880 Lower Valley Road
Atglen, PA 19310
Phone: (610) 593-1777; Fax: (610) 593-2002
E-mail: Info@schifferbooks.com
Web: www.schifferbooks.com

For our complete selection of fine books on this and related subjects, please visit our website at www.schifferbooks.com. You may also write for a free catalog.

Schiffer Publishing's titles are available at special discounts for bulk purchases for sales promotions or premiums. Special editions, including personalized covers, corporate imprints, and excerpts, can be created in large quantities for special needs. For more information, contact the publisher.

We are always looking for people to write books on new and related subjects. If you have an idea for a book, please contact us at proposals@schifferbooks.com.

**Other Schiffer Books by the Author:**

*Welcome to Weaving: The Modern Guide*, ISBN 978-0-7643-5631-5

**Other Schiffer Books on Related Subjects:**

*Natural Dyeing with Plants: Glorious Colors from Roots, Leaves & Flowers*, Franziska Ebner & Romana Hasenöhrl, ISBN 978-0-7643-5517-2

*Threads Around the World: From Arabian Weaving to Batik in Zimbabwe*, Deb Brandon, ISBN 978-0-7643-5650-6

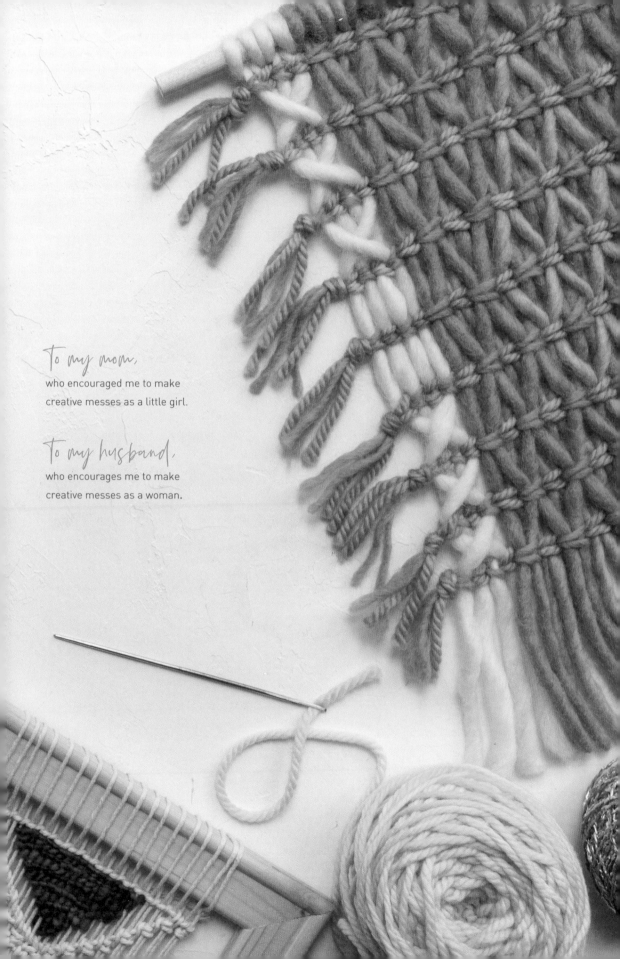

To my mom,
who encouraged me to make
creative messes as a little girl.

To my husband,
who encourages me to make
creative messes as a woman.

Contents

# Introduction

Ready to take your weaving skills to the next level? This book was made to help modern weavers expand on their beginning knowledge through intermediate and advanced techniques and projects.

When I turned in the materials for my first book, *Welcome to Weaving: The Modern Guide* (if you haven't read it yet, you should), I went a little overboard. After a few months of trying to squeeze everything into 160 pages, my editor and I realized that what I'd created was actually two books, in terms of the learning sequence and the number of skills and techniques.

What you hold in your hands is the guide to building on your foundation. I believe that ending with a beginner's book about weaving is like cutting off a love story before the main characters even meet.

Since writing my first book, I've continued to connect with thousands of weavers around the world through our love of yarn and looms. I'm constantly amazed and uplifted by the fact that weaving is a universal language. It's practiced around the world in many ways by people of all walks of life. Every person has their own narrative to share that propels the craft forward, and I love watching this medium continue to evolve. I have been interviewing weavers in different countries and learning about the unique methods that are used in their cultures, and keeping a list of exciting advanced techniques to practice and share one day. The opportunity to write this second book was the answer to my prayers!

The more I learn about weaving, the more I fall in love with it, and my love is constantly growing because there is SO MUCH to learn. Between the two books, the story of weaving continues to draw you along the creative process, from beginner to advanced.

## How to Use This Book

Now that you've learned the basics (plus a little more) about weaving from my first book, *Welcome to Weaving: The Modern Guide*, you should feel confident with your skills. This book was created to go beyond being an introduction to weaving, and to provide a reference guide as your skills grow. You know the difference between "weft," "warp," "loom," and "shed" and how to keep your sides straight. You have a loom and are comfortable creating shapes. You have an uncountable amount of projects and designs to try, using just the basics! That's where this book comes in.

Even though this book is an extension of my first book, I included some of the foundational techniques in case you need a convenient refresher, or a reminder. Believe it or not, it is possible to forget whether to go over or under! I've also included directions to build yourself a loom because it gives you freedom to tackle projects as big or small as you want . . . and some of the projects at the end of this book are BIG.

Although you are welcome to jump around between chapters, this book is created to reflect the creative process. Section 3 teaches intermediate and advanced techniques. These techniques come from all over the world and are a wonderful way to go from dipping your toe in the craft to diving deeper. Each technique includes a list of projects that use it later on in the book, projects that will expand your creativity as you think outside the box.

The most common way to use modern weaving is by creating a tapestry to display your work, and that's what section 4 is about. Each tapestry has a theme and refers back to any techniques that are used, so that you can revisit them if you need to. Even if you follow each tapestry step by step, your finished piece will turn out unique based on the yarn, sett, and colors that you choose.

The projects section of this book, section 5, is a jumping-off point to provide ideas for you to create usable items with your skills. These projects include a general explanation on how to manipulate the resources that you have. Although the specific woven designs are not explained in as much detail as the tapestries, they are meant to be used as a beginning point for you to create your own designs and follow the tutorial as inspiration to create something unique.

If there's anything I've learned from chasing down new weaving techniques and connecting with weavers across all skill levels, it's how vital creativity is in our lives. Creativity is more than making something with our hands. It's an important part of self-care. My hope with these books is to do the heavy lifting of curating terms, tricks, and techniques so that you can make the most of your creative time and simply enjoy the act of making.

In the project gallery on the next page, you will find inspiration by looking over the completed design for each project included in this book.

The techniques and projects between my two books will set you up to be able to weave anything you have in mind. I created this series as a tool that you can refer back to again and again. The techniques and projects will continue to answer your needs in different ways as your weaving skills progress. Keep the books close to your loom to open up when you want to follow a specific method or just to find inspiration if you are faced with a creative block. There is something for everyone, no matter what your weaving style is!

## Learn to Make . . .

Need some inspiration to get you started? Here are the exact tapestries and projects you will learn how to create later on in the book. You can jump ahead to follow each one's step-by-step instructions, or continue reading to learn about specific techniques and terms beforehand.

Page 101

Page 105

Page 111

Page 115

Page 119

Page 125

Page 131

Page 134

Page 136

Page 144

Page 142

Page 147

Even advanced weavers need to brush up on the terminology and basic techniques every now and then. I've included these first sections to review the foundational knowledge so that you won't be lost if you don't have my first book, or if you do have both, you won't need to flip back and forth between the two. Plus, there are advanced-level tips about the basics here, as well as some foundational techniques that start to apply only when your weaving becomes advanced. I recommend reading through section 1 and section 2 so that you are completely ready to level up your skills!

# Make a Loom

If you feel up to it, go ahead and make a loom yourself! It is often a cheaper option and takes only three easy steps. I made my first loom because I couldn't find all the features I wanted combined in one design. It is still my favorite loom to weave with.

You can use many household items to create a usable loom. The key to success is finding a sturdy frame of some sort that won't buckle or lean when your warp is wrapped tightly between the edges.

Gather supplies. You will need a stretched canvas (this one is 18" × 20"), a ruler, a pencil, a screwdriver, some finishing nails, and a hammer.

A large, cheap option is to use a canvas stretcher. You can pick one up at your local craft store. There are many different sizes to choose from, although many times they already have canvas stapled on the frame. Simply remove the canvas by picking out the staples in the back. If you are extra handy and possess woodworking tools, you can also make your own frame with a few pieces of wood and some screws. This gives you full control over the size of your loom. Just make sure that your edges are square.

*(Step-by-step pictures on following page)*

2. Use your screwdriver to dig out the staples that hold the canvas in place in the back.

3. Remove the wooden frame from the canvas.

4. Use a ruler to draw two parallel lines ¼"–1" apart on each of the farthest edges of your frame.

5. Use a ruler to mark points ⅓" apart, alternating between the two lines so that every other point is placed above and then below along the width of your frame.

   Alternating the placement of the nails will make it easier to warp the loom later on and will keep the frame from cracking because too many nails are in one row.

6. Add nails. Use a hammer to pound a small nail into each mark, and then go back to lightly angle the nails on both sides of the loom away from each other. This added step helps hold the warp strings in place during any strenuous lifting or pulling while you weave.

7. Repeat on the far side of the frame so that the nails match up straight and your loom is complete. farthest edges of your frame.

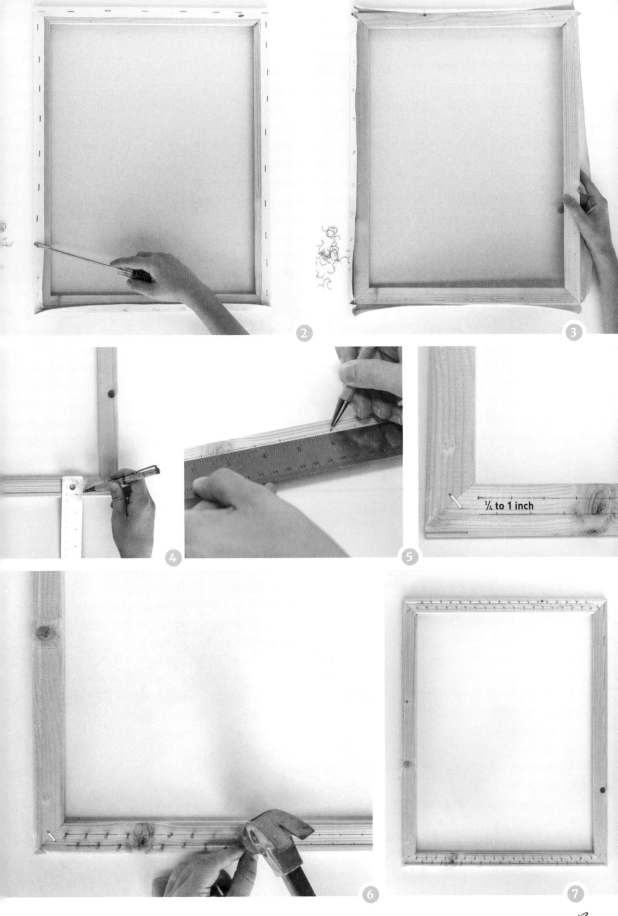

¼ to 1 inch

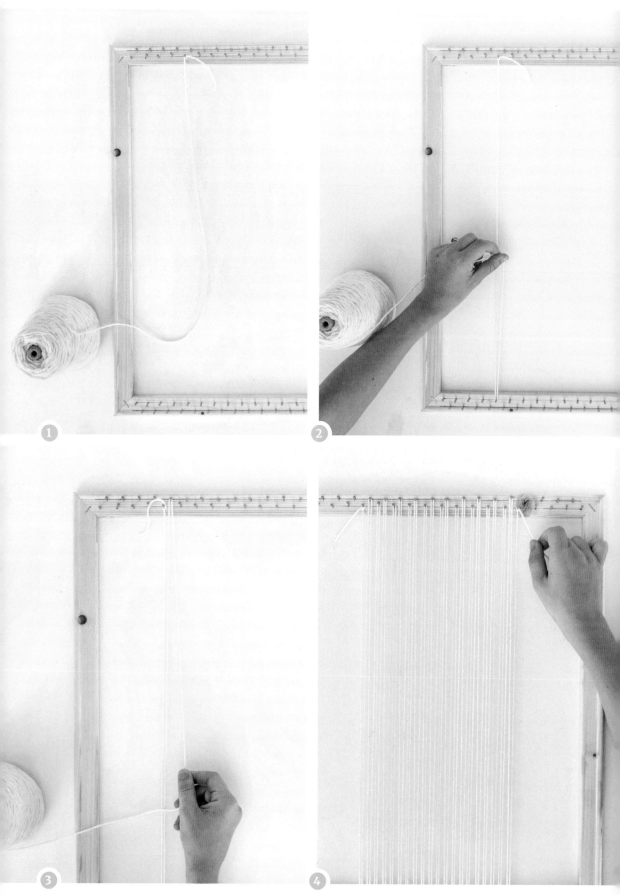

# Warping

## Planning

You do not need to premeasure your warp string. Simply pull string off the cone/ball as you go. If you have a specific space or rod you want the tapestry to fit, create a contained warp. Before warping, plan how wide you want your tapestry so that you can measure how many notches on your loom you need to use.

Choosing the correct warp string is important. It needs to be strong, a consistent thickness, hard twisted, smooth, and not too thick to withstand the constant tension and friction as you pass weft rows through and beat them into place. The best warp string is made from cotton.

**Advanced Tips**

Do you have a loom that has notches instead of nails? Although this type of loom requires special tools to make, so you might not be able to make one yourself, it also provides even more flexibility for warping. With notches you can "double warp," which creates a high-sett, or high-density, warp. Or you can space out your warp as far as you want.

Warp your loom while it is lying flat on the ground or a table. This will make it easier to maintain even tension as you pull the warp string back and forth across your loom. Begin and end with knots oriented on the top side of your loom (the side farthest away from you). This will always result in an even number of warp strings to work with, for easier hanging once you remove the tapestry from the loom.

1. Count the number of notches (nails) that you need to span your desired length, and center this number in the middle of your loom. I want my finished tapestry to be 10" wide, which comprises 20 notches on my loom. I find the center 20 notches and will have nine leftovers (unused notches) on either end. Take the end of your warp string and tie a knot around the top far-left notch that you will be using for your project.

2. Carry the thread down to the bottom of the loom to wrap it around the parallel notch on the other end. Be sure that each warp string is straight and not diagonal.

3. Carry the thread up to the top of the loom again to wrap it around the next notch and then back to the bottom.

4. Repeat these steps until you reach the last notch at the top of your loom. Tie a knot and cut off the string.

## MAINTAIN EVEN TENSION

The key to keeping good tension while warping is not to let go of the warp string as you are carrying the thread up and down from the top to the bottom. Maintain the same amount of pulling pressure as you wrap the thread around each notch, and tie the last knot to hold the last warp string as tight as the rest.

The warp should have an even tension across the loom. To tell if your warp has proper tension, place your hand on various parts of the warp. The strings should have enough give for your hand to sink an inch or two before resisting and spring back when you remove your hand. Warp with good tension will act like guitar strings when you strum it. There will be a short vibration and not much give or sag. Uneven tension across the loom will result in difficulty weaving and ripples within your tapestry once it is removed.

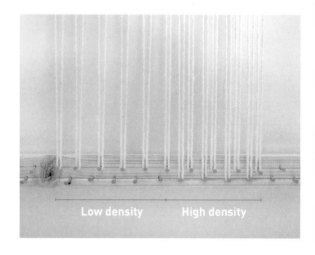

Low density      High density

A low sett is perfect for beginners and for quick projects using thicker wefts. Your weave will be looser, have a lower tension, and have a simpler design. To achieve low-sett warp, loop your warp string around every other notch on the loom. Each slip will have one warp string—either exiting or entering—and only every other notch will have a loop around it.

## LOW-DENSITY VERSUS HIGH-DENSITY WARP

The epi (ends per inch) of your warp determines how thick the yarn that you use as warp is.

The sett of your warp determines how closely your warp strings will be to each other.

A higher sett will allow you to add more detail to your tapestry. It takes longer to weave and has a higher tension, but you can create smoother angles for shapes and curves. To achieve a high-sett warp, loop your warp string around every notch on the loom. Each slit will have two warp strings—one entering and one exiting, and each notch will have one loop around it.

## EXTRAS

Mix up your warp to achieve unique effects. Use a contrasting-colored warp string across the entire loom or just one stripe for a pop-up color as it peeks through the weft rows.

You can also mix high- with low-sett warping on the same loom. This is helpful if your project needs detail only in one area of your tapestry and you want the rest to be loose and quick. If you mix warp densities, pay special care to your tension because your weft will be tighter in areas with a higher-warp sett.

# Advanced Tip

These instructions are for a standard-sized loom for tapestries and other small- to medium-sized projects. Sometimes you need a loom that is a special size, or built for extra-large projects (such as the rug project on page 136). If you can't find a canvas frame that is big enough, I recommend using larger pieces of wood to create a frame, and then simply use these instructions for how to space your nails across the top and bottom. You can find plans for an adjustable loom on my website at www.hellohydrangea.com. The size of your loom can be as big as you want!

# Weaving Upside Down

Many weavers work differently, but I recommend the method of weaving upside down. Start from the bottom of your loom and work your way up. With this method the twining header is the first row you complete because it will end up being at the top of the tapestry when it is hung up.

Designing a weave is more flexible if you begin at the tapestry's top instead of with the fringe that hangs off the bottom. You can always add more length to your fringe, it's true, but it is important to have a fixed amount of length reserved for the top loops. You don't want to run out of space by leaving the top for last!

In working from the top of the design to the bottom, there is another problem. Due to a little thing called gravity, your rows will fall down if you push them upward, and it will be harder to maintain consistent tension. When weaving upside down, on the other hand, you beat down the rows. Gravity will be on your side.

This is why I recommend weaving upside down.

# Time to Weave

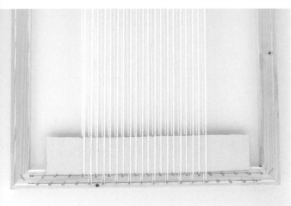

Now that your loom is warped, it's time to begin weaving. However, before you weave your first row, make sure to leave enough warp length at the beginning of the tapestry to knot and tie onto your rod when you are done, about 2". You can use a cardboard guide to help keep the first row straight by cutting a 2" strip of cardboard and weaving it onto the bottom of your loom before adding the twining header rows.

# Section 2

# FOUNDATIONAL TECHNIQUES

# Twining Header

Level: Beginner | Projects: Almost All

The twining header is the first stitch you will complete. It will hold the top of your weave in place once it is completed and removed from the loom. Using a worsted cotton similar or the same as your warp strings will keep the twining header minimal in width, so that it does not distract from the main design. The purpose of the twining header is to evenly space your warp strings, to prepare them for the rows of stitches that will come afterward, and to stabilize the next few rows of stitches to prevent them from sliding down as you weave and once the tapestry is removed from the loom.

1. You will need to begin with a length of string that is about six times the width of your pre-determined tapestry, so measure from the first warp to the last warp six times.

2. Fold this length of string in half to find the center, and then hook the center behind the first warp string on the left so that both of the tails lie in front of the loom.

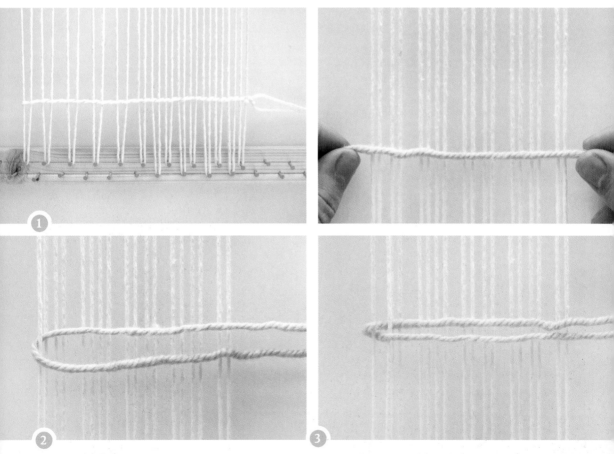

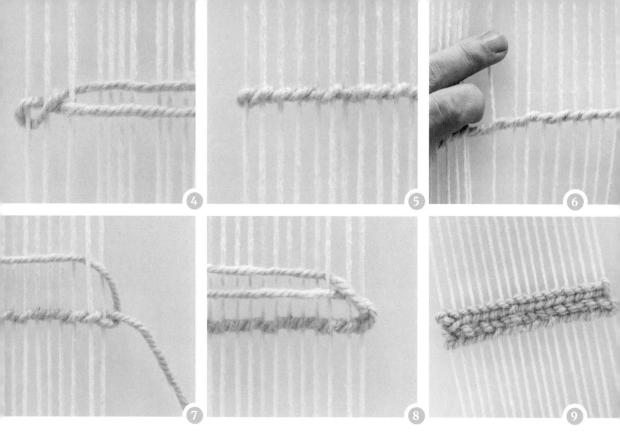

When you place the two tails perpendicular to your warp from left to right, you will see that one is on top and the other is on bottom. Begin by slipping the top tail behind the second warp string on the left.

Next, take the bottom tail, bringing it over the top tail and slipping it behind the third warp string on the left. Now the top tail is on the bottom and vice versa.

Repeat these steps until you reach the last warp string on the right. It doesn't matter if your rows of twining arch up. You can beat them into a straight line at the end.

When you reach the end, hold the top and bottom tails together in one hand and use the other hand to walk across your warp strings, one by one, removing any obvious slack in the twining header. This will make sure the warp strings are spread evenly and provide extra durability.

Finish up the full row of twining by turning around and going back to make a second row. To turn around, drop the top tail down, over the bottom tail. Slip the bottom tail behind the second warp string on the right.

Now you have a top and a bottom again. Continue the same twining stitch by bringing each bottom tail over the top and slipping it behind the next warp string in line until you reach the end of the tapestry again.

A twining header is usually made of one or two rows, but you are welcome to complete more. Once you have reached the end, tie the two tails together. Use a beater or a comb to push down the two rows of twining until they make a straight line, about 2–3" from the bottom of your warp strings.

# Plain Tabby Weave

Level: Beginner | **Projects: Almost All**

After the twining header is complete, I always begin with a few rows of plain weave, or tabby, to further stabilize the end of the piece and keep the warp strings evenly spaced for future rows of stitches. The basic tabby is the essential weaving stitch. With the tabby, you can create shapes and cover a lot of space swiftly. It is a flat weave, so the designs created with tabby are two-dimensional, but it is also the foundation for many other tabby stitches that create texture. You can learn more about the different stitches that use tabby as the base at the beginning of the next chapter.

## Weft versus Warp Dominant

Tabby works with every type of fiber; however, depending on the thickness of your fiber, there will be differences in the effect. A yarn thinner than your warp will make your rows extra tight and create a "weft dominant" weave, meaning your warp strings will be completely covered up with rows of tabby. If you use yarn thicker than your warp strings, the rows will be looser, and your warp string will be visible as it holds the thick fibers in place. That's a "warp dominant" weave.

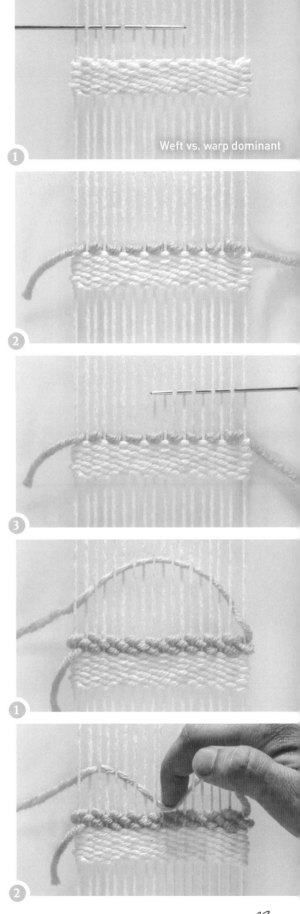

1. The plain weave consists of guiding your weft over one warp string and then under the next.

2. When you reach the end, you will notice that the weft ends either over or under the last warp string.

3. To turn around, hook the weft in place around the last warp string by beginning over (if you ended under) or under (if you ended over).

*That's it!* You just learned the most important technique in weaving. You can create almost anything, just by knowing how to plain weave.

## Bubbling

Level: Beginner | **Projects: Almost All**

When your weft is guided straight through as a plain weave, it risks pulling the edges of your tapestry in, especially as you get farther into the middle of the loom, where the warp tension isn't as strong. To stop this from happening, it is essential (VERY IMPORTANT) to relax the tension of your tabby weave with a process called bubbling.

1. As you guide your weft through the warp, keep it at least 2–3" above the last row in an arc shape.

2. Once you have completed a row, push down weft until it touches the last row every 2–3" to make small hills before beating the row down.

Weft vs. warp dominant

# Beating Down Your Rows

Level: Beginner | **Projects: Almost All**

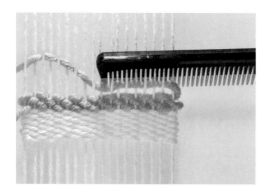

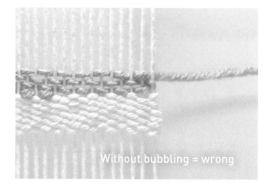

Without bubbling = wrong

Once you have created hills of loose yarn for the bubbling technique, the last step is to beat down your rows. You can use your fingers, a comb, the edge of your shuttle, a beater, or just a regular hairbrush!

Without bubbling and beating, your weft will be pulled too tightly, causing the edges of your weave to be cinched in, and your rows will be too tight to stack properly.

## Advanced Tip

An extra tip to make sure you have edges that are as straight as a ruler: beat down only the first inch of your weft, on the side that folded around your selvedge warp string first. This lets you slow down and make sure that your weft that is looped around the last warp string stacks perfectly in line with the edge of the row below it. If it's too loose, it will stick out farther than the last row, and if it's too tight, it will pull in tighter than the last row. If you get the first inch of each row exactly where it needs to be, your edges are sure to be straight!

With bubbling and beating, your weft will interlock with the warp in a natural, smooth process as each row is neatly stacked one on top of another.

# Advanced Tips

Did you know there's an extra step between "bubble and beat" that helps maintain your tension even more? After you have bubbled your weft, strum the back of your fingers across the warp strings. If you look at the row from the side after strumming, you can see that it has settled your weft over and under the warp strings instead of separating a gap between them. This step helps your tension so that the sides of your tapestry don't pull in.

As projects get more advanced, especially with different patterned techniques, try to tuck your tail down through rows that are the same color so that they don't show up between any gaps in the rows. Sometimes this can't be done, in which case, tuck it through only a small number of rows to minimize any show-through.

## Tucking Tails

When you begin a new fiber, color, or section, you will have to decide how to secure the beginning and end of each row so that they do not come apart when the tension of your warp is released from the loom.

1. When you begin a new row of tabby, leave a tail. You can use a regular overhand knot on the first warp string.

2. The tail should be at least 1" long and will be woven in first or will be left to tuck in at the end. The end of the tail should always exit toward the back of the tapestry.

3. When you reach the end of the last row, thread your needle down through the rows of tabby, parallel to the warp string.

4. Pull your yarn down with the needle. Make sure that the needle exits out the back of the tapestry.

5. As long as you tuck your tail through only the rows that are the same color as the yarn you have just worked with, your ends will be completely hidden and securely attached. The tails on the back of the tapestry will be trimmed later on.

When you get to the end of a section and are ready to move on to a new material, color, or location, you should immediately take care of the leftover tail from your current yarn before continuing. Tucking it in now will save you a lot of time and frustration when you reach the end of your tapestry!

# Weaver's Knot

Level: Beginner | **Projects: Almost All**

A question that new weavers often have is, "How do I know how much yarn to cut for my technique?" If you are using a needle, you will need to pull the yarn through the warp, so you don't want a length that is obnoxiously long. As you continue weaving you will be able to predict how much to cut off more accurately, knowing how much will get used. The important thing to know is that if you do run out of a length of yarn, you can always add more—and that is where the importance of the weaver's knot comes in.

When you reach the end of your yarn but want to continue, either with the same color/material or different, you can use the weaver's knot for a secure, seamless, almost invisible connection.

1. Leave a 2–3" tail from the yarn you are currently working with and cut a new length of yarn. Fold the two tails of both pieces of yarn about an inch in and hook them onto each other.

2. The end of the new length of yarn is going to wrap around the back of the old length of yarn and down through the center.

3. Pull both ends tight to complete the knot. This knot is secure enough that you can cut the two tail ends almost flush to the knot, or you can leave the two tails for added security and tuck them parallel to the row, exiting out the back of the tapestry to be trimmed later on.

4. To further hide the connection, and minimize the bulge, position the knot head behind a warp string so that it is hidden completely.

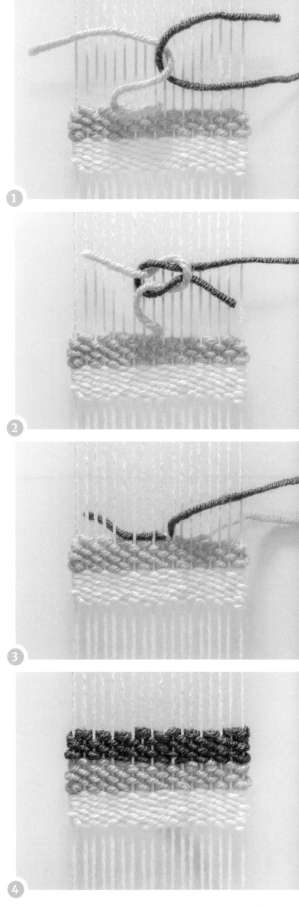

# Hooking Wefts

Level: Intermediate | Techniques: Pibione, p. 69; Deflected Double Weave, p. 89; Krokbragd, p. 87

This simple trick is used in many advanced techniques such as pile weave, pibione, and krokbragd if you are working with two wefts that span the width of the tapestry together to create patterns. When your wefts reach the selvedge warp they can either hook around the last warp, which might mess up the pattern, or hook around each other. By hooking around each other they are less conspicuous and the pattern is still intact.

1. If the pattern calls for the bottom weft to end underneath the last warp string, and it also needs to begin underneath the last warp string the next time it works across the tapestry, guide it over the top warp string and then underneath the warp string to hook it on the edge as it continues through the pattern.

2. If the pattern calls for the bottom weft to end over the last warp string, and it also needs to begin over the last warp string, guide it under the top weft and then underneath the warp string before continuing the pattern.

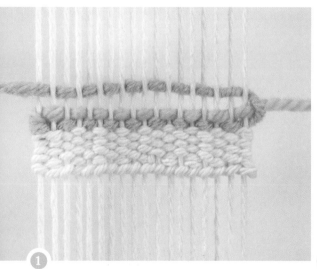
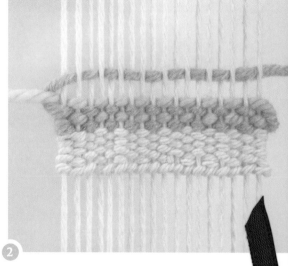

# Floating Selvedges

Level: Intermediate | **Techniques:** Waffle
Weave, p.84; Twill, p.64

This is another simple trick that is used in
many advanced techniques such as waffle
weave, deflected double weave, twill, and
overshot if you are working on a pattern that
floats over more than one warp string at a
time. When your weft reaches the selvedge
warp in the middle of floating over warp
strings and needs to turn around and begin
the next row floating over the same warp
strings, you have to sacrifice the pattern on
the very last warp string. This is called a
"floating selvedge" because it doesn't follow
the pattern and is used solely as a hook for the
weft to set up to continue the pattern.

1. You can use the floating selvedge as
   you are finishing a weft row, depending
   on the pattern. For example, if the
   pattern calls for the weft to float over
   the last warp string, and then also
   begin over the first warp string . . .

2. . . . instead, you can break the pattern
   as you are finishing the row by hooking
   the weft under the last warp string.

3. If the pattern calls for the weft to float
   over the last warp string, and then also
   begin over the first few warp strings . . .

4. . . . instead, you can break the pattern
   as you are beginning the row by
   hooking the weft under the first warp
   string.

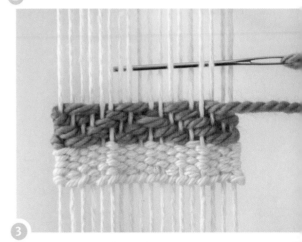

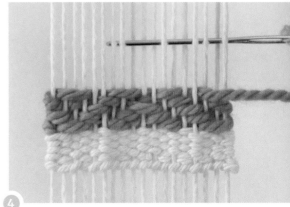

# Pick-Up Sticks and Heddles

## Shed Stick

As you are weaving with the tabby stitch, you might start to feel like the process takes a long time to guide your shuttle device over and under each warp string. There are a few ways to speed up the process!

One way is to use a pick-up stick, also known as a shed stick. The "shed" is the space that is created when half of the warp strings are lifted together, allowing your shuttle device to quickly move the weft through, instead of going over and under each warp string individually. You can use many things for your shed stick; a ruler, a strip of cardboard, or an actual shed stick/sword. The stick should be about an inch thick and the width of your tapestry, or the width of the section that you are weaving.

Simply guide the stick over and under your warp strings once, as it is lying flat. When you flip the stick up vertically, it holds the shed between your warp strings open for you to guide your yarn through one row. Then lay it flat again as you turn around and guide your yarn back through the next row normally, weaving "counter-shed" by manually going over and under each warp string.

As your tapestry gets longer, the tension of your warp strings will get tighter, making it harder to use a shed stick. Eventually you will need to discard the pick-up stick because forcing your warp strings to separate may result in them coming unhooked from your loom.

# Heddle

A single shed stick is great for quick and easy weaving, but it only solves the problem of opening the shed for your weft to travel through one way. What about picking up the opposite warp strings for speedier weaving as you come back through the next row? That is where heddles come in handy.

A heddle is often used in large floor looms or rigid heddle looms to easily pick up certain warp strings for faster weaving, the way shed sticks do. However, unlike shed sticks, you can have an unlimited number of heddles attached to your warp. Instead of simply guiding your stick through the warp and opening the shed, you have to lift each warp string with leashes, which are sewn onto a leash stick.

1. Instead of creating individual leashes for each warp string, you can sew on your heddle with a continuous string. You will need a dowel and some yarn.

2. Guide your yarn from the right of the tapestry to the left, going under each warp string that you want your heddle to pick up. Tie one end of the string onto your dowel.

3. Begin by pulling up the yarn after the first warp string under the yarn by about 2".

4. Twist the yarn 180 degrees clockwise.

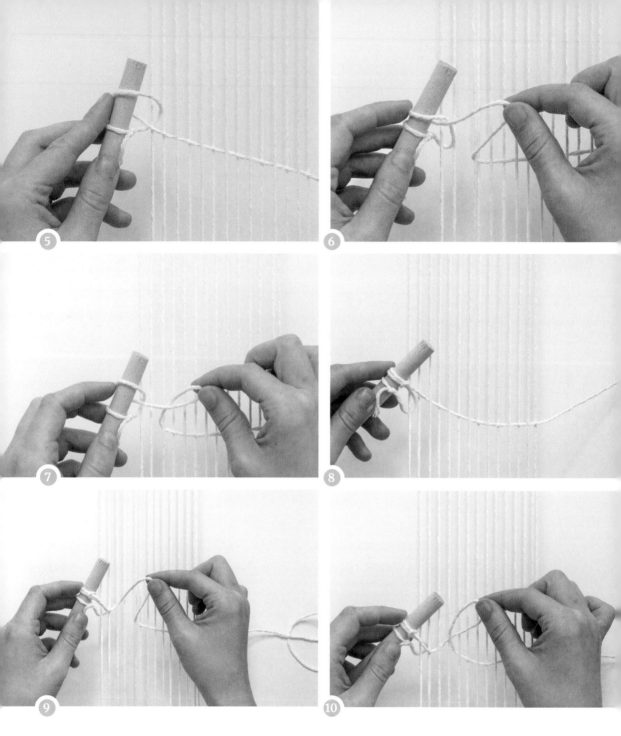

5. Slip the dowel through the loop.

6. Pull a second length of yarn from the same area, after the first warp string by about 2".

7. Twist the yarn 180 degrees clockwise and slip the dowel through the loop.

8. Pull the end of the yarn so that the two loops are pulled together.

9. Pull a length of yarn after the second warp string under the yarn, about 2".

10. Twist the yarn 180 degrees clockwise.

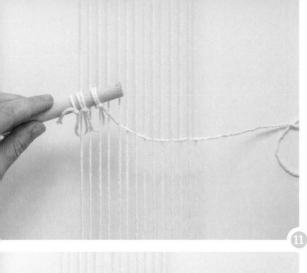

11 Slip the dowel through the loop.

12 Repeat this process until each warp string under the yarn has two following loops slipped onto the dowel. Tie a knot to secure. As you add more loops to the dowel, you will need to slide previous loops farther down the dowel to make room to add more.

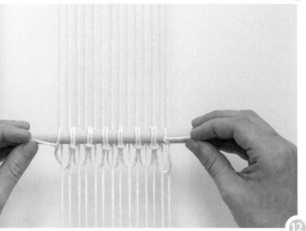

The heddle will easily fall when your loom is standing up, so hold it in place by tying the ends onto the shed stick above, or to the top of the frame loom.

To use the heddle and the shed stick together, simply flip up the shed stick and guide your weft through, then flip the shed stick back down and pull the heddle up to guide your weft back.

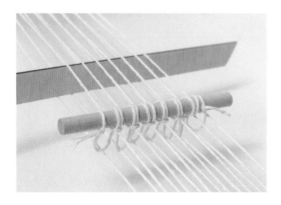

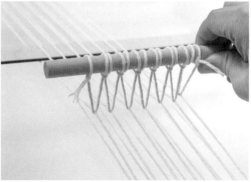

# Removing the Tapestry from the Loom

It's finally time to reveal your tapestry and remove it from the loom. This is my favorite part! Many weavers who leave the job of tucking in their tails until the end dread this last step because it can be a daunting job after they've already been working on a piece for many hours. Did you tuck your ends in as you went? If you did, then the last part is super easy! The key is tucking those ends in as you go, for minimal work at the end.

1. Start by turning your tapestry over and double checking that all of your tails are tucked in, including the first row's twining header.

2. Now all you have to do is trim each tail that is sticking out of the back of your tapestry, knowing that they are secure and won't come undone once the weave is cut off the loom. Your back should be clean and flat.

3. It's time to cut the warp strings. Make sure everything is finished the way you want, because once the warp is cut there is no turning back. You can't fix any mistakes or add anything to your design. Cut only the warp strings that will be at the bottom of your tapestry, leaving the top warp strings as loops.

4. When the warp is cut, pull the loops above the twining header off the loom.

5. The very last element to secure your weave is to add a regular overhand knot on each of the top loops, right above the twining header.

Once your warp is cut, your tapestry will be at its most vulnerable, which is why it is so important to have a twining header at the top and a hem stitch at the bottom, with your design sandwiched in between. The twining header is essential for your weave at this point because it holds all of your rows in place from the top. It is so satisfying seeing all the little extra steps pay off in the end.

If you finished with fringe rya, you can leave the bottom warp strings because they will be covered by a wall of fringe. However, if you want a straight border on the bottom of your tapestry, you can tuck each warp string up through the back of your tapestry, just as you do when tucking in ends.

Your loom has finished its job with this project, so you can set it aside until you're ready to warp it up for your next tapestry.

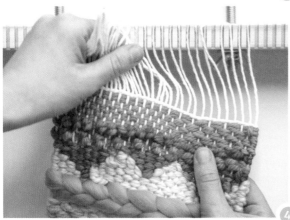

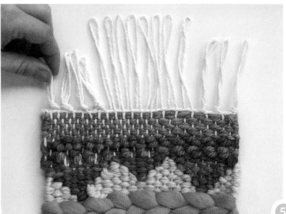

# Finishing a Tapestry without Fringe

Level: Beginner | Projects: Delicate Details, p. 114

If you want a project without warp strings hanging from the bottom of your piece, this is an easy way to secure the ends and hide any fringe on the top or bottom.

1. Finish your weave by securing the edges. You can do this with either a hem stitch or overhand knot to cinch the warp strings in pairs along the border. My preference is to finish with a row of twining for an extra-smooth edge.

2. Use a needle to tuck the warp strings back up into the back of the weave, up through a few rows of weft, parallel to the warp strings within.

3. Tuck all warp strings up across the width of your weave. This is especially helpful if you want edges that aren't straight, such as curves or angles.

4. Cut any extra tails from the warp strings from the back.

5. The view from the back should be clean with no fringe, and any signs of the warp strings should be tucked along the backside.

6. The view from the front should be a seamless straight border without any sign of the bottom warp strings.

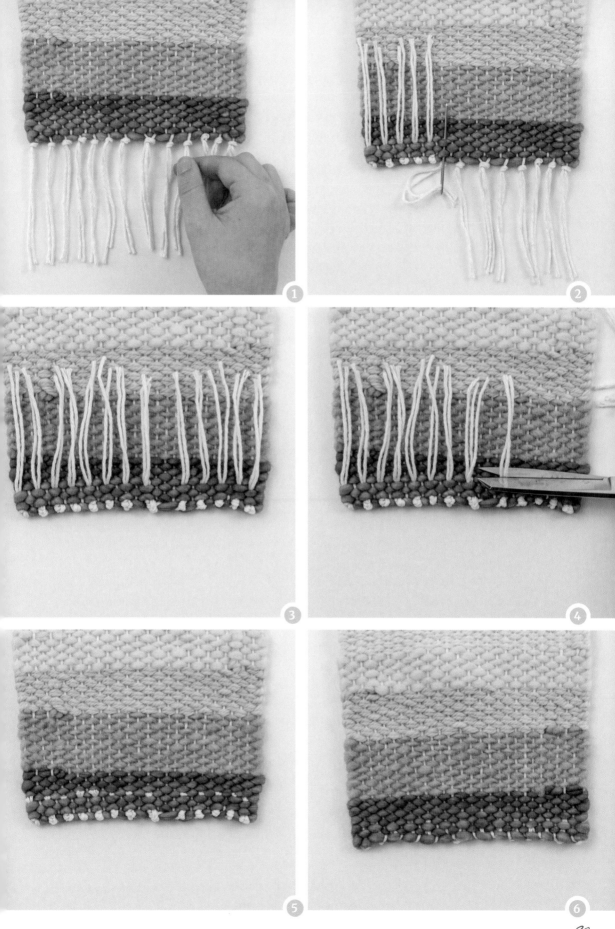

# Finishing with Wrapped Top

Level: Intermediate | **Projects: Fringed Patterns, p. 124**

Add a polished edge to the top of a hanging tapestry by wrapping a woven section around the dowel. This can be done the full width of the tapestry, or in slits along the top, depending on the style you choose. This effect takes some planning because it should be the first part that you weave on your tapestry, so have your rod picked out first so that you know how much space you will need to wrap around it.

## Advanced Tip

For a seamless edge, use a color of yarn that matches the hue of the dowel or rod you are using. Your rod needs to be straight to be wrapped in yarn (no irregular sticks).

1. Before you begin weaving, measure the circumference of your dowel so that you know the length to weave your top section. Begin with a twining row and then add as many rows as you need to complete the length before moving on to the rest of your tapestry design.

2. Once your tapestry is complete, cut it off the loom. Lay your tapestry flat so that the backside is facing up. Use a needle to tuck the warp strings back up into the back of the weave, up through a few rows of weft, parallel to the warp strings within.

3. Cut any extra tails from the warp strings from the back.

4. Place your rod in the center of the top section and wrap the weave around the rod.

5. Use the same yarn that you wove the top section with to add a running stitch so that you can connect the top edge with the bottom edge, securing the wrap around the rod.

6. The view from the front should be a seamless tapestry all the way to the edge, with a wrapped section at the top and a rod exiting out either end.

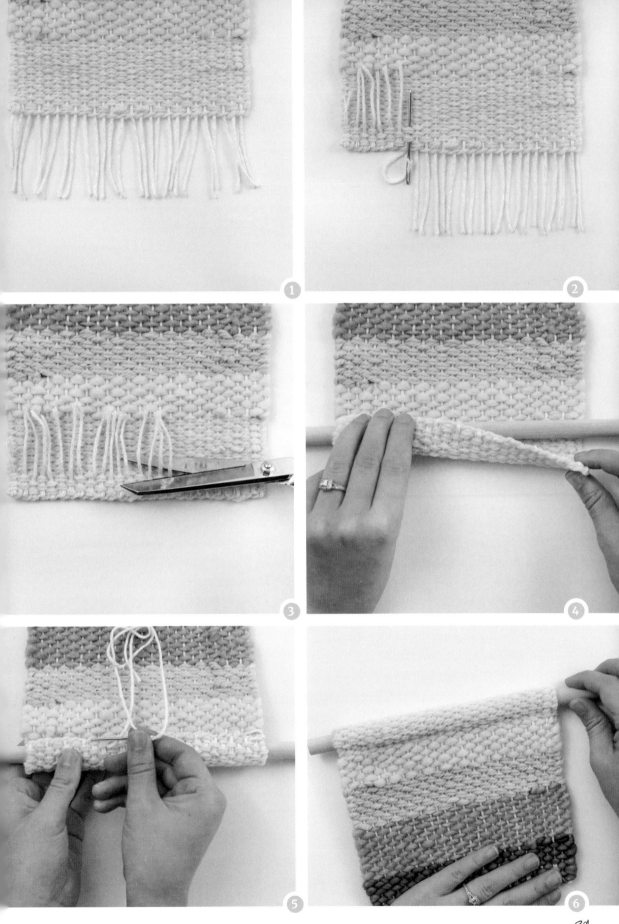

# Finishing with a Hanging Sleeve

Level: Intermediate

If you don't want a rod to show at the top at all, you can weave pockets, or a sleeve to hang the rod behind your design so that it appears to float on the wall. This effect takes some planning because it should be the first part that you weave on your tapestry, so have your rod picked out first so that you know how much space you will need to wrap around it.

## Advanced Tip

The sleeve will be hidden on the backside of your weaving, but part of it can be spotted from the side, so choose a color to blend into your wall. For less bulk at the top choose a thin, strong dowel.

1. Before you begin weaving, measure the circumference of your dowel so that you know the length to weave your top section. You will need one section of yarn to create sleeves on either edge of your tapestry with at least a 2" area open in the center so that your rod is exposed and can be hung on the wall. The top of each section should begin with a twining row, then add as many rows as you need to complete the length before moving on to the rest of your tapestry design. You should also add a twining row to the top of the open section, where the top of your actual tapestry design begins.

2. Once your tapestry is complete, cut it off the loom. Lay your tapestry flat so that the backside is facing up. Use a needle to tuck the warp strings back up into the back of the weave, up through a few rows of weft, parallel to the warp strings within.

3. Cut any extra tails from the warp strings from the back.

4. Place your rod in the center of the top section so that it spans the width of your tapestry but does not extend beyond the edges. Wrap the sleeves around the rod. Use a yarn that is the same color as your warp or weft so that it doesn't show from the front. Sew a running stitch to secure the sleeves behind the tapestry so that the fold at the top is completely hidden on the back, wrapped around the rod.

5. You can also sew the edges of the sleeves to the edge of the tapestry to prevent the rod from slipping out of the sides.

6. The view from the front should be a seamless tapestry design all the way to the edge, with a slight bulk at the top that appears to float on the wall.

*Here's what the front versus back looks like for these two ways to finish the top of a project.*

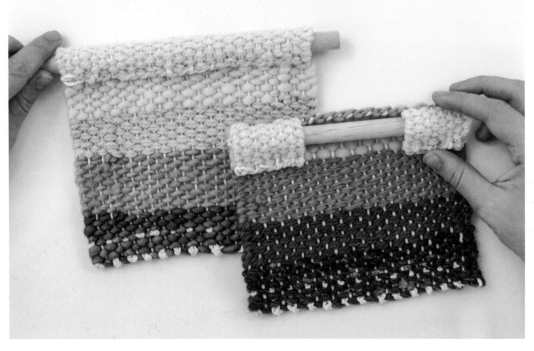

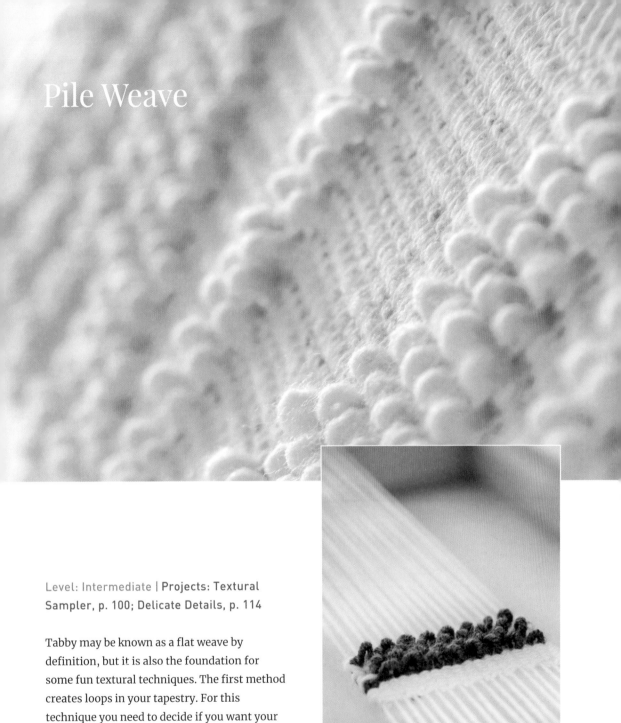

# Pile Weave

Level: Intermediate | Projects: Textural
Sampler, p. 100; Delicate Details, p. 114

Tabby may be known as a flat weave by
definition, but it is also the foundation for
some fun textural techniques. The first method
creates loops in your tapestry. For this
technique you need to decide if you want your
loops to be nice and even or carefree and
offbeat. If you want them to be universally the
same size, you will need to find a long, smooth
rod such as a pencil or a knitting needle that is
the size of the loops you want to create.

ABOVE | Pibione, taught on page 69, is a form of pile
weave laid out in patterns.

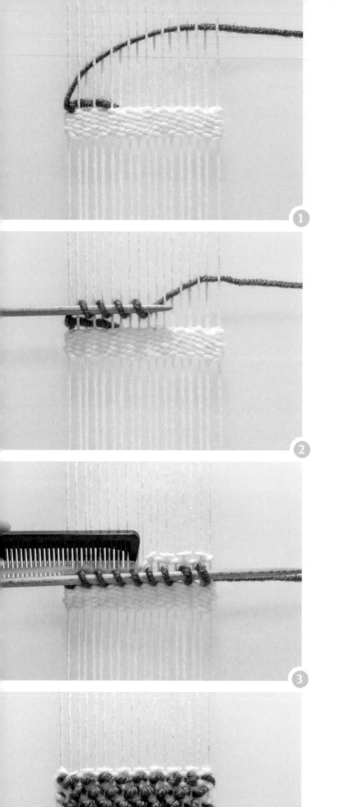

Begin by tying a knot and weaving in the tail. Then create one row of loose tabby, but don't beat it down yet.

To maintain your tension during this technique, always begin from the side that is continuing from the last row, and work your way to the side that has the excess tail. Gently pull out enough yarn from between two warp strings on the row to slip the end of your rod through. Do this again for each loop that you want to create, pushing your rod through as you slip the loosened yarn over the end.

When you reach the end of the row and all your loops are slipped over your rod, follow with a full two rows of yarn before gently pulling the rod out of your loops. Beat down the full two rows to hold your loops in place.

You can decide how thickly you want your loops piled up, which depends on the frequency that you pull the loosened yarn out. For a thick, tight-loop pile, pull out yarn between every or every other warp string. For a thin, loose-loop pile, pull out yarn between every three or more warp strings.

# Twisted Floaters

Level: Intermediate | Projects: Delicate
Details, p. 114

This fun technique combines three combinations of plain weave, including tabby,
floating tabby, and loops, for an effect that
shows off the texture of your material. It works
best when you use loosely spun roving or two
to three strands of yarn at once. The looser the
material you use for your rows, the more your
twisted floaters will look like long pom-poms!

Before you begin, decide how far apart you
want your twisted floaters to appear, and count
the number of warp strings that will be
between them. You will also need to know how
long you want your twisted floaters, and count
the number of warp strings they need to cover.

1. Complete a regular row of tabby over
   the number of warp strings that will
   separate your twisted floaters.

2. As you come to the gap where your yarn
   will float over a few warp strings, twist
   the tail of the yarn before continuing on
   to another set of tabby to separate your
   twisted floaters. Keep the twisted part
   loose so that it expands as it floats over
   your warp strings. Continue to alternate
   with plain tabby and a twisted floater
   until you reach the end of the row.

3. Stack at least two rows of plain tabby
   above the floater row, and beat each
   down to hold the twisted floaters in place.

4. If you choose to do more than one row
   of twisted floaters, separate your
   floaters so that each one is centered
   between two floaters from the previous
   twisted-floater row.

# Draping

Level: Intermediate | **Projects:** Monogram Door Handle Decor, p. 134

Draping is an effect that looks similar to fringe, although both ends of the string are connected to the surface of your tapestry, instead of hanging loose. There are a few ways to create draping.

## Tuck Edges

One of the easiest ways to create draping is done after you have finished weaving a section.

Use the larkshead knot to add fringe onto a row of draping.

Cut a length of yarn and use your needle to tuck the two tails down through your rows, just like you do when tucking in ends.

With this technique you can adjust the length of the drape by pulling the back tails or the front drape.

## Sagging Float

A second way to create a draping effect uses the same weft material you are already weaving with.

Begin weaving a regular tabby row, allowing your weft to float over a number of warp strings that you want the drape to cover.

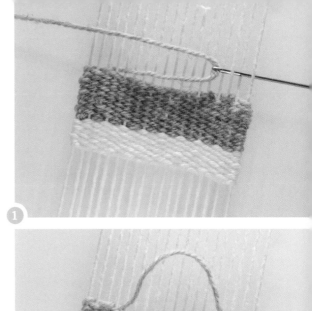

Let out excess material so that it sags and drapes before tucking it into the shed again.

Continue with regular tabby rows after the drape.

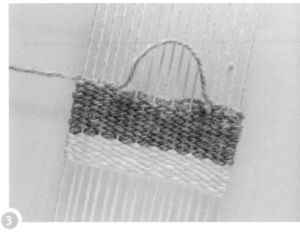

You will not be able to adjust the drape once you continue weaving rows. To keep the height of your rows even, you may need to make up for the empty space that a sagging floater leaves in your row.

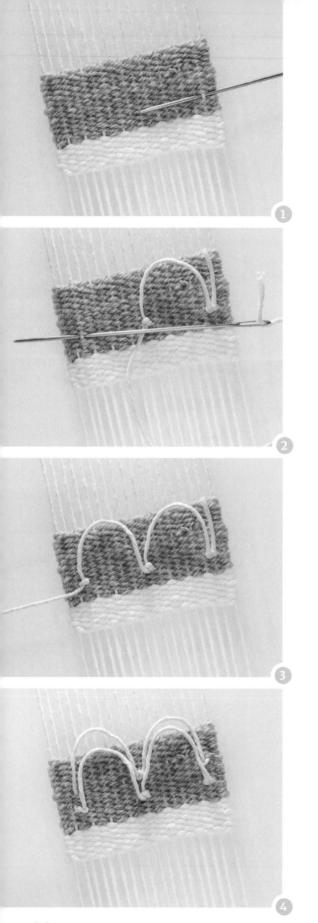

## Knotting

The last way to create drapes is similar to tucking edges, but it allows you to create continuous scallops and use a thicker material.

> Begin by tying a knot onto the warp string, between the existing weft rows.

> Allow your yarn to drape to your desired amount before tying another knot onto another warp string farther down.

Continue draping and knotting. If you want to add a second layer of drapes, and your material is thin enough, tuck the tail from the last drape through a few rows of tabby and then begin the knotting and draping again.

When you want to stop simply tie the last knot and trim your tails.

# Looped Rya

Level: Intermediate | **Projects:** Textural Sampler, p. 100; Free-Form Hoop, p. 110

Creating fringe with tails that loop together is a whimsical technique that can add lots of extra volume to your tapestry quickly. This method looks especially good tucked underneath a textural soumak or below regular tabby knots for a layered-loops effect. There are two ways to create looped rya.

## Uncut Bundles

The first way to create looped rya is by making the individual bundles that you usually do with regular rya, but not cutting the tails. Decide how long you want your rya fringe in advance because you will not be able to shorten them in the future without cutting off the loops.

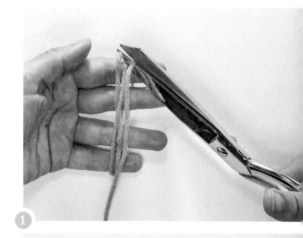

1. Use your hands or a book to wrap your yarn in equal bundles, two to four loops each.

2. Each length will be looped twice with two tails.

3. Fold the length of bundle in half with both of the tails on one end, and center it around a pair of warp strings before tucking the ends around the back and up through the center of the warp strings, in a regular ghiordes knot technique.

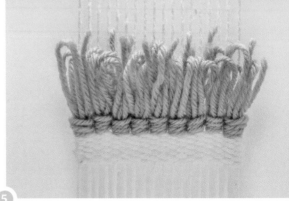

**④** As with all rya, follow up with a full pass of tabby after each row.

**⑤** Among the loops, each bundle will have two straight, cut tails.

## Continuous

If you don't want the extra straight, cut tails in your loops and don't want to create individual bundles, you can use a second method. This technique uses a continuous piece of yarn, so you don't even have to cut it off the skein until you are done!

1. Begin by tying your yarn onto a warp string.

2. For each rya loop, make a sideways U shape, facing the direction that you are moving across the tapestry with the continuous tail on top.

3. Use your fingers to lift the second warp string from the end, and grab the continuous tail before pulling it back through and down.

4. You can pull on the tail to tighten the loop and make the loop as short or long as you want.

5. Move on to the next pair of warp strings by making another sideways U shape to repeat the process. Pull the tail through the second warp string.

6. Continue this method as you move across the warp strings.

This technique is vulnerable to being easily pulled out until you add at least two rows of tabby above it to hold the loops in place. Remember that you are weaving upside down, but when you flip your tapestry right side up, the rya loops will look like regular rya with a knot on top and the loops below. This technique looks especially good when you use more than one continuous yarn at a time to make the loops.

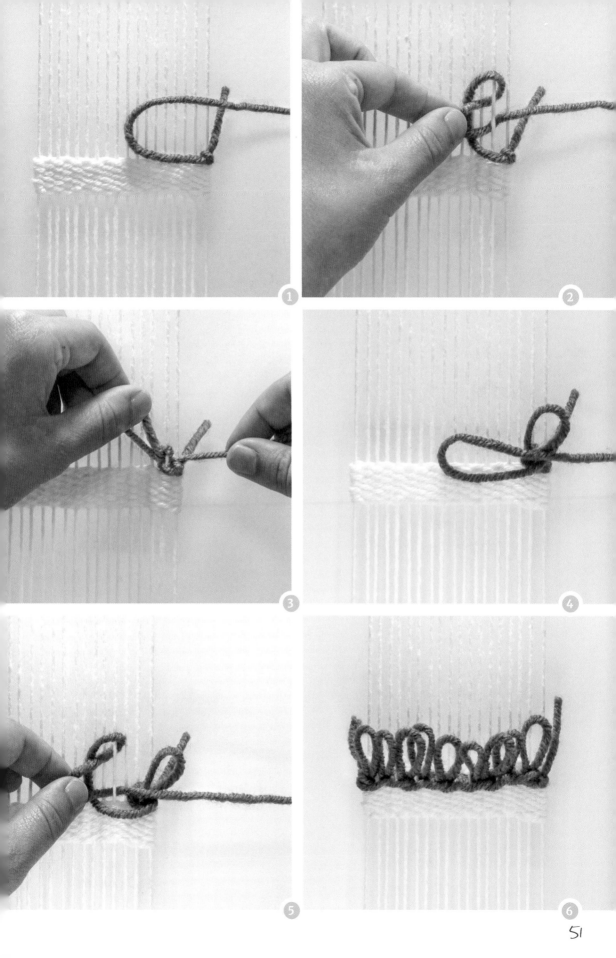

# Hem Stitch

Level: Beginner | **Projects: Almost All**

The very last technique you will complete on your tapestry while it is still on the loom is also possibly the most important. It is called the hem stitch, and it will keep your weave from falling apart when you cut the warp strings free. Can you imagine all of your hard work coming apart? It could happen if you don't complete the hem stitch!

The hem stitch uses a needle and yarn to tightly pull pairs of warp strings together and hold the border in place.

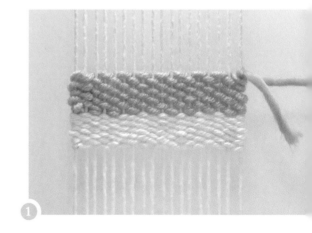

Before you begin the hem stitch, you always need at least two rows of tabby, especially if your last stitch was any type of rya. Tabby is important for the hem stitch to grab onto. You can even complete two quick rows and then go straight to working on the hem stitch with the same continuous yarn. Tie a knot on the first string and weave in the end.

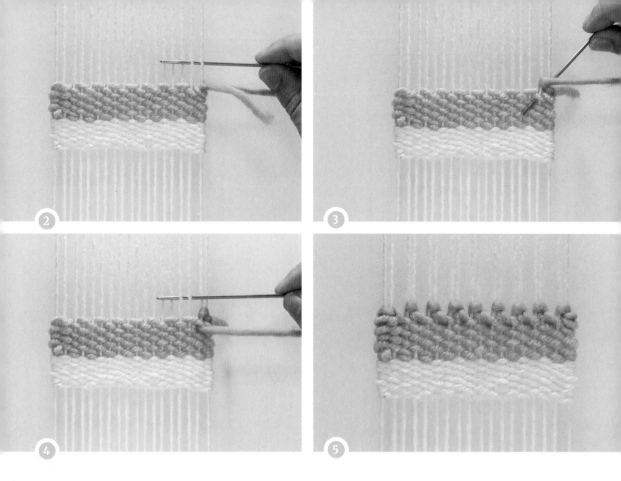

② Guide your needle behind the first two warp strings and pull the yarn through.

③ Then, guide it behind the same two warp strings, but this time come up from underneath two rows of tabby, right after the second warp string that it went behind. Pull the yarn tightly through.

④ Guide the yarn behind the next two warp strings and follow the same steps of pulling it through and then coming back up through two rows of tabby.

⑤ Continue all the way across your tapestry. Knot the end and tuck it in.

Each knot should encompass a pair of warp strings. As you pull the string under the tabby rows, the pair of warp strings is pulled tightly together. This will close up your warp so that the weft rows are held in place and won't fall down when your tapestry is cut off the loom and hung from a rod.

# Gradients

One of my favorite weaving techniques is creating gradients with yarn that fade from one color to the next. They add a showstopper element to any tapestry! Creating gradients requires a little math, but believe me, it's worth it.

To achieve a gradient effect, the ratio of the new color needs to grow with each new length of yarn as the ratio of the old color decreases. You can complete a gradient with only two colors, but if you want your gradient to be subtler you need to use a color spectrum with more colors. For example, if you want a subtle gradient from yellow to red, you need to find two or more colors of yarn that fall between the two colors, so that your sequence is, for instance, yellow, peach, orange, coral, red. If you want your gradient to be more gradual, you will need to lengthen the amount that you weave with each ratio, no matter how many colors you use.

# Tabby Gradient

Level: Intermediate

Thin yarns are best to use. Each color of yarn that you choose should be the same thickness. You can even use cotton embroidery floss to get a great color spectrum without investing in large quantities of yarn.

Try creating a simple gradient by using only two colors of yarn. Cut lengths of yarn and divide them into bundles. Each bundle will have a different amount of colors. The number of one color versus the other in each bundle is understood as a ratio. For example, three reds and one blue is a ratio of 3:1 in the bundle. Always think of one color as the first number and the next color as the second number to keep yourself organized.

As the mixture of separate strands in each bundle is woven, the strands will randomly twist and the different colors of yarn will peek through at different times to create a slightly stippled effect.

Measure your tapestry width four times and then cut 10 lengths of each color at this size.

1. Begin with a bundle of four strands with a color ratio of 4:0; that is, all four strands are the first color. When you get to the end of the first bundle of lengths, simply use a weaver's knot to add the next bundle and continue.

2. The next bundle of four strands will be a color ratio of 3:1, so that three strands are the first color and you introduce one strand of the second color.

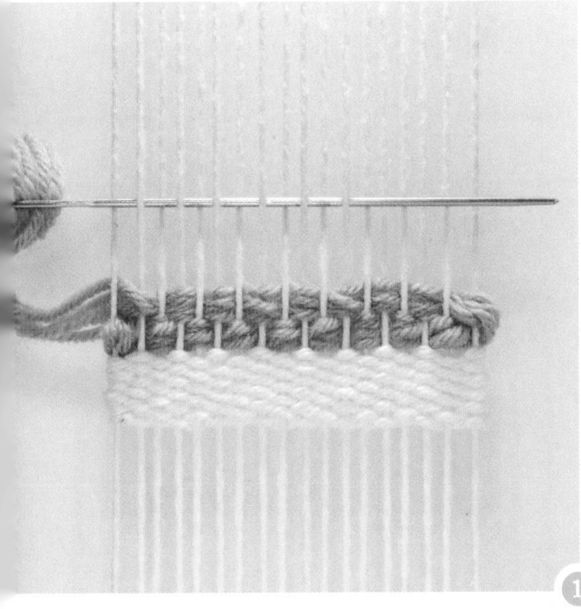

1

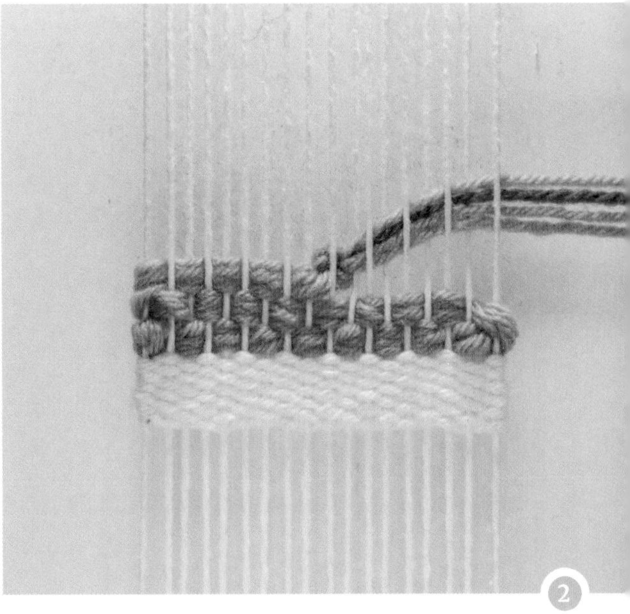

2

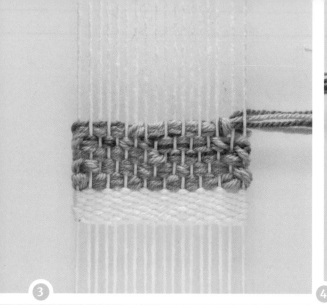

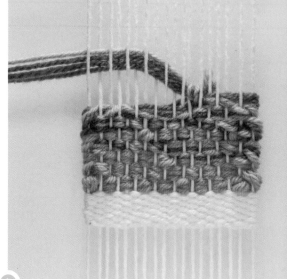

③ The next color ratio is 2:2, so that two of the strands are the first color and two are the second color.

④ Now the ratios will decrease in the second color's favor. The next ratio is 1:3, so that only one strand is the first color and three of the strands are the second color.

⑤ The last ratio is 4:0, so that all four strands are the second color.

⑥ Your first gradient is now complete. If you wish to continue, simply follow the same steps but introduce a new color so that the ratios begin increasing again.

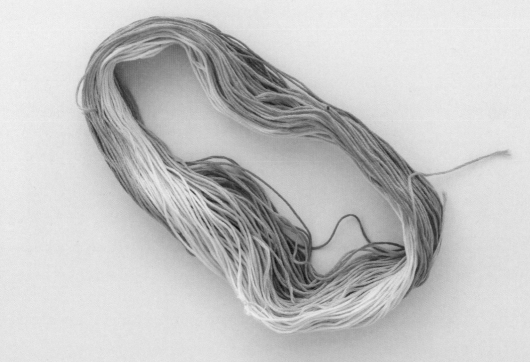

## Rya Gradient

Level: Intermediate

Tabby gradients and rya gradients are very similar, although rya gradients require more yarn and even more planning. You will use the same techniques so that the ratio of the new color grows with each bundle of yarn. It is very helpful to measure out your bundles of rya beforehand.

A gradient with only two colors will still use a ratio of 4.

ABOVE | Embroidery floss is a great material to test gradients with because it is thin, so the effect appears to smoothly fade from color to color.

The first bundle of four strands has a color ratio of 4:0, so all four of the long strands are the first color. The second bundle has a ratio of 3:1, so three of the strands are the first color, and you will introduce one strand of the second color. The third bundle has an equal ratio of 2:2, so two strands are the first color and two strands are the second color. The fourth bundle has a ratio of 3:1, so three strands are the first color and one strand is the second color. The last bundle has a ratio of 0:4, so all the strands are the second color.

Once you have all of your ratio bundles measured, go through and cut each bundle into smaller bundles of lengths 3–4" long. Now that your bundles are organized and cut, your job is easy.

1. Begin with the strands from the first ratio bundle. You can choose to make each knot equal or make them varied by grabbing two to five strands of yarn at a time to tie rya knots onto your warp. Continue until you reach the end of the row. As always, add a few rows of tabby to hold the rya knots in place before continuing onto the next row.

2. Continue until you reach the end of the first ratio bundle. Now grab two to five random strands of yarn at a time from the second color ratio bundle to tie rya knots onto your warp. Some of your rya knots will be all one color, but some will have strands of the second color. Don't forget to add a few rows of tabby between each row of rya.

3. When you reach the end of each bundle, simply grab the next bundle and continue.

4. The different colors will appear randomly based on which pieces of yarn you grab each time, but the ratio in the bundles will stay true and your gradient will slowly appear.

5. When you are done, you can choose to leave your rya knots longer for a waterfall gradient effect, or cut them close to the tapestry for a carpeted effect. To see the gradient the best, create a carpeted rya. Flip the loom over and give your fringe a haircut. Have a comb nearby to even out the fringe from all angles.

6. When you are happy with the cut, your rya gradient will be complete.

# Twining Patterns

Level: Advanced | Projects: Delicate Details, p. 114

Twining patterns are commonly seen in rug weaving or backstrap weaving, but they are also fun to experiment with on a frame loom. Twining is a weft-dominant technique, so when you stack more than one consecutive row of twining, your warp will be completely hidden. You will be using the same basic technique as you learned in the twining header, but when you use more than one color and strategically twist your yarn in different ways, you can create pixelated effects.

You can go around each individual warp string, or a group of two to three warp strings at once. Depending on the color that you want to be seen in the pattern, you can twist the yarn so that your chosen color wraps around the front. It helps to have a pattern to follow so that you know which color should be shown and which should be hidden.

1. Begin with a single slip knot to tie your two colors together with a 1–2" tail. Just as with twining, you will be twisting the two yarns around your warp strings so that one goes around the back while one goes around the front.

2. Creating a regular twining row with two different colors will result in a candy cane stripe.

3. When you reach the end of your row, twist the two strings until the front string is the color that you need to begin with and then begin undertwining. Overtwining is the regular practice of twining. Undertwining means that instead of the bottom strand going over the top and behind a warp string,

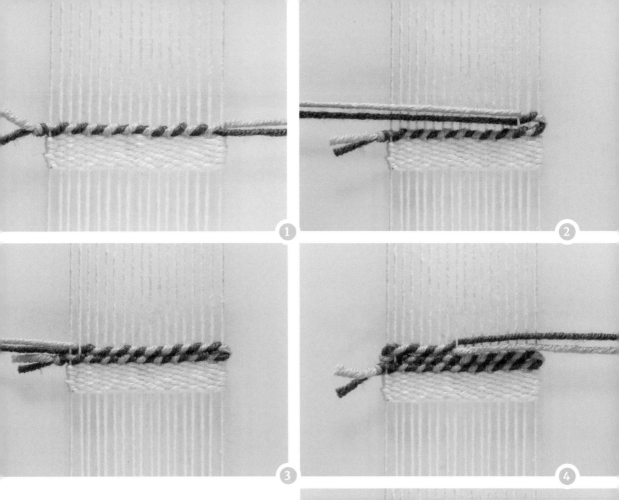

the top strand will go below the bottom and behind a warp string.

4 Undertwining allows you to change direction while still having your twining angle in the same direction, which is important for patterns.

5 The important thing to remember when twining patterns is that whatever strand goes behind the warp string will be hidden, while whichever color goes in front of the warp string will show.

A single twist will send the current color to the back and bring the second color to the front. This is the same technique you used for the twining header. When you want to have the

same color repeat again on the front, twist your yarns twice so that the current color remains on the front and the same color remains on the back.

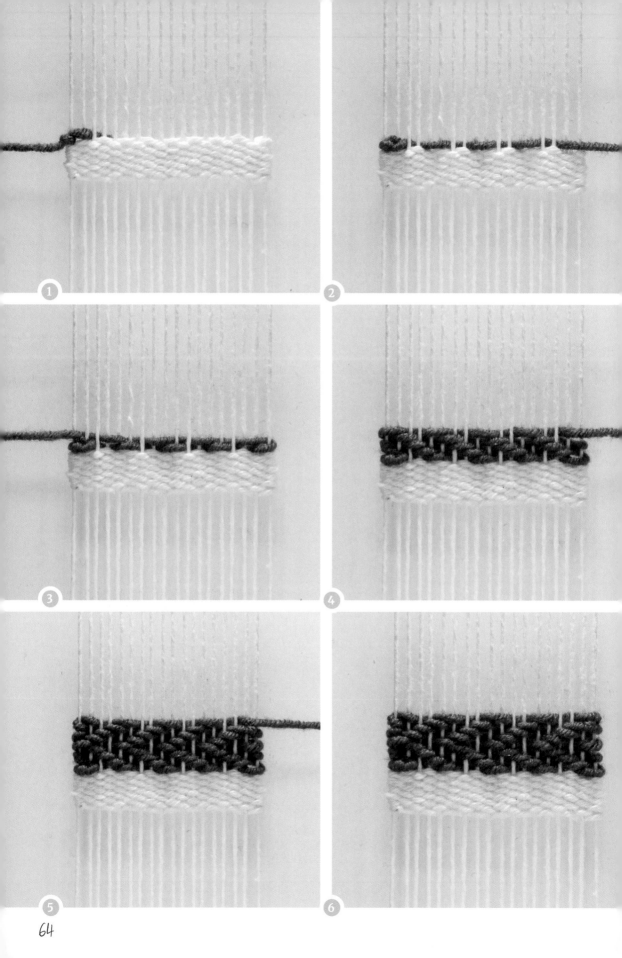

# Twill

Level: Intermediate | Projects: Diamond Twill Rug, p. 136

## Chevron Twill

Twill techniques are similar to tabby because they move the weft horizontally across the warp, but in a way that makes a subtle pattern. When a weft passes over more than one warp in a row, it is called a floater. Twill techniques can be simple but can provide a unique element to your tapestry with as little effort as a regular tabby.

1. Begin as you normally would for a tabby stitch by tying your tail on the first warp string and tucking it in. However, as you move across the warp, go under two warp strings, over two warp strings, under two, etc., just like floating tabby instead of single tabby.

2. When you reach the end, even out your tension, just as you would with tabby, by bubbling and beating the row down.

3. When you turn to begin the second row, you will continue going over and under two warp strings at a time, but stack your weft one warp string to the left of the row below, so that the exposed weft appears to make a diagonal pattern.

4. To make your pattern clearer, beat down each row tightly so that the weft rows blend together. You can also use a looser, thicker yarn than your warp strings so that the exposed weft pattern is easier to see.

5. You can continue stacking one warp string to the left for a completely diagonal pattern, but if you can, also angle your rows back the other direction for a chevron pattern. After you have completed four or more rows, stacking them each one warp string to the right, begin stacking your weft one row to the left so that the exposed warp makes the diagonal appear to go the other direction.

6. You can then complete four more rows before stacking one row to the right again. Continue this technique and your chevron pattern will emerge!

## Diamond Twill

Twill is a technique that is practiced mostly on a rigid heddle loom, because complex patterns are easier to create when heddles can automatically pick up the warp strings in the correct sequence for each row, and a large area can be quickly woven. However, that shouldn't stop you from trying a more complex pattern out on your frame loom! The results are very rewarding.

For more-complex patterns, the weft floats over and under in a specific repeated combination, such as over two and under three, or over one and under four. The combinations are endless and can get very complicated. Complex twill patterns require a mapped outline to follow, called a draft, until the weaver learns the sequence. (Search online for "houndstooth, diamond, or herringbone twill weave" to find more patterns!) Below you'll learn how to make a diamond pattern. You can follow along with this pattern in more detail, using the draft.

I will walk you through the first two rows.

1. Begin on the far-left warp string, tie a knot, and tuck the tail. Begin by going over three, under two, over one, under two, and then over three again, and repeat the sequence until you get to the end. That wasn't too hard, right?

2. Now, locate the last time you went over three warp strings in that row. For the next row you will go under one warp string right in the middle of those three warp strings. Since you know that you will be going under one warp string in that spot, count the sequence from that spot back to the end of the row. Under one, over two, under three, over two, under one, etc., until you reach the end.

3. Guide your weft through the pattern of the sequence that you just counted out. When you reach the last point of the pattern that you went over three with the last row, you should go under one, just as you planned!

4. You can use this method of locating a section in the pattern and counting the sequence back to where your continuous yarn is waiting to help you through the draft.

It doesn't matter where you begin on the draft, but once you have a row completed it is important to pay attention to the sequence. As long as you stack your rows correctly so that the sequence matches up with the draft, your pattern will emerge. The first two to five rows are always the hardest because you don't yet have an existing pattern woven on your loom to follow.

Sometimes the first and last one to two warp strings on each row require you to break the sequence. This is because you can't end a row and begin a consecutive row both going over (or under) the same warp string. You need to anchor your row by hooking your yarn around a warp string. If the sequence matches up so that this happens, simply sacrifice the pattern either on the last warp string on the finished row or the first warp string on the new row, and then continue the sequence correctly.

Twill is easier to follow if you draw your design on grid paper beforehand.

columns = warp strings →→→

rows = r

- - - - = repe

*Now that you know how to follow a draft to create a complicated twill pattern, try making your own!*

Creating a pattern with the twill stitch will yield different effects depending on the yarn you choose to use. At the bottom I used a thin, tightly wound cotton, and on the top I used a thick, loosely spun wool. You can choose what thickness to use, but I find that it works best to use a yarn that is the same thickness as the distance between your warp strings.

Now that you know how to follow a draft to create a complicated twill pattern, try making your own! Use some graph paper to map out your own design. The vertical columns represent the warp strings, and each horizontal row represents the weft. Draw and shade-in your design to mark where to guide your yarn over the warp. The best patterns float over only one to four warp strings at a time; any more than that and your weft will sag out of place without the support. Try containing your pattern to a number of cells that is 12 by 12 or less so that you can repeat the pattern and it won't be too complicated.

## Pibione

Level: Intermediate |
**Projects: Cross-Body Fringed Bag, p. 144**

Pibione is a beautiful, delicate technique that is native to the small island of Sardinia in southern Italy. The name means "grapes" in Italian, which is fitting because it creates small bumps, called grains, that make a subtle pattern on the surface of the tapestry. A similar technique from Canada is called boutonné.

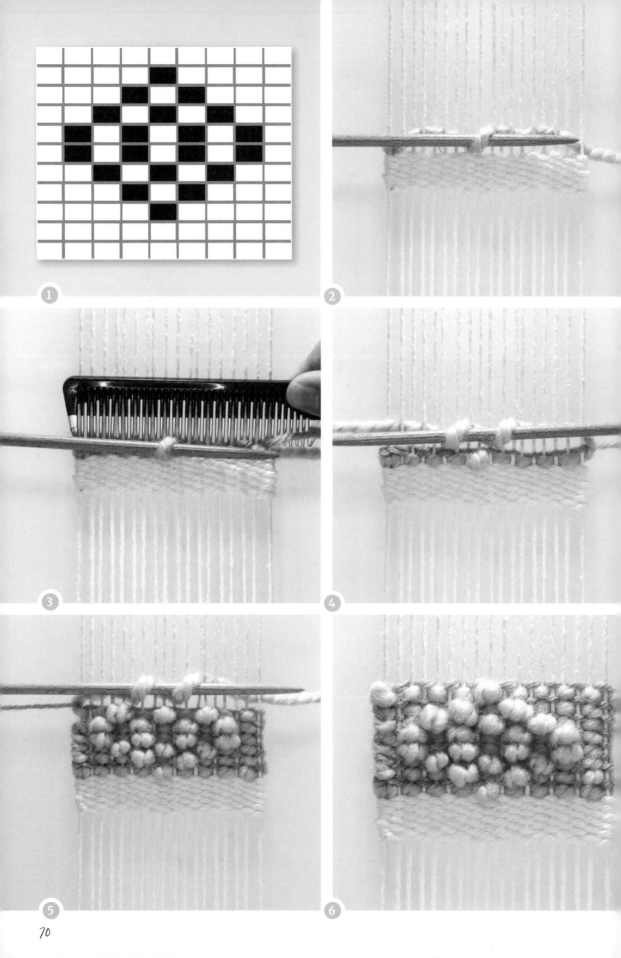

This technique is the same as the pile weave technique. Each grain is pulled out of a warp row and looped around a smooth, straight rod. The location of the grains is different in each row, so that when the piece is completed, a pattern has formed.

1. You can try this folk technique yourself. The first step is planning out your design on grid paper, as you did with the twill pattern, to help you keep track of where to loop your weft. Each vertical line represents a warp string, and each horizontal square represents your weft. Use dots to mark your pattern. You will need a thin, smooth, straight tool to wrap your weft around. A dowel or a knitting needle will work.

2. To follow your pibione draft, weave a row of weft through as a plain tabby but keep it loose and do not beat it down. Move from the fixed side of the weft to the direction of the tail and use your fingers to pull out pieces of your weft over different warp strings to wrap around your rod. Wrap around the rod between warp strings only if the location is marked with a dot on your grid. If there is no dot, leave the weft to continue as a regular, flat tabby.

3. After each row, beat down your pibione row and complete one or three rows of regular tabby to hold it in place. The number of tabby rows needs to be odd so that when you begin with the pibione row again, the grains line up like pixels. Then you can carefully slide the loop tool out and begin working on the next row of loops.

4. The loops that you pull out will correspond to the boxes on your grids.

5. Using two different wefts is similar to the pick and pick technique. When you turn around, remember to hook the two yarns at the end of each row, exactly like the hooking method shared on page 28.

6. The pattern that will emerge from your loops is subtle and textural.

# Supplementary Wefts

A creative way to add patterns and pictures to weaving is by adding a supplementary weft. The extra yarn is not actually woven into the tapestry, the way traditional tapestry-weaving patterns are, with rows of tabby, hatching, and interlocking. Instead a yarn specifically chosen for the pattern floats between two tabby rows, hooking either on the foundational weft or the warp to hold in place. If the supplementary weft is cut off, the foundational tabby would still be plain woven.

Supplementary wefts are done in many different ways, and the patterns can become very complex and time consuming. Because of this, they are usually saved for large looms with heddles. However, you can also try some supplementary weft techniques on a frame loom!

# Overshot

Level: Intermediate | Projects: Woven Vest,
p. 147

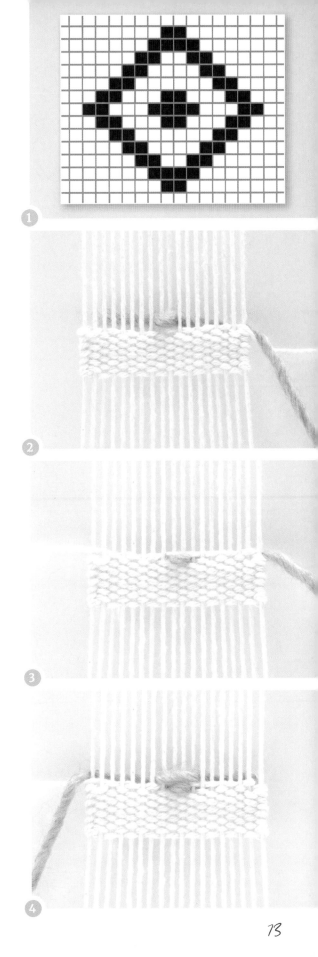

One of the most common supplementary weft
techniques is called overshot. With overshot
the supplementary weft spans the length of the
tapestry. Usually the pattern is repeating so
that it can easily cover a large area quickly.
When the supplementary weft is not needed for
the pattern on the surface of the tapestry, it
floats on the backside.

1. Once again, you can plan your draft in
   advance with graph paper, where the
   columns represent warp strings and
   the rows are rows.

2. Begin weaving regular tabby with the
   background yarn. Follow the first row of
   the draft to add the supplementary weft
   over any warp strings in the pattern, but
   leave it to float behind any warp strings
   that are not highlighted in the pattern.
   To hook the supplementary weft in
   place at the end of the row, drop the
   supplementary weft over the top of the
   foundational yarn.

3. Weave a row of plain tabby weave,
   using the foundational yarn.

4. Add the next row of supplementary weft.
   At the end, drop it over the top of the
   foundational yarn to hook it in place.

⑤ Continue alternating between tabby and supplementary wefts until the pattern is complete.

⑥ If you turn the tapestry around, you will see that the pattern is reflected in reverse on the backside. Wherever the supplementary weft was not used in the pattern, it will float behind in a reverse of the pattern.

## Krabbasnar

Level: Intermediate | Projects: Delicate Details, p. 114

Krabbasnar is a Scandinavian folk technique that uses a supplementary weft method in vertical rows to create patterns. The columns may be long or short and may change color, but each column is a separate length of yarn.

Unlike overshot, krabbasnar does not span the width of the tapestry in the back. It hooks in the background weft as soon as its time in the front is over, so that there is miniscule pattern showing in the back. The width of the columns of the supplementary weft usually covers only a few warp strings.

① Begin as you did with overshot by weaving regular tabby with a background yarn and then adding the supplementary weft so that the tail hangs down in the back.

② Weave a row of plain tabby weave, using the foundational yarn.

③ Bring the supplementary yarn back over the two warp strings in the column. The row of background weft will hold it in place as it hooks under the tabby row and then comes back to the surface.

④ Continue alternating between rows of supplementary weft and background tabby, hooking the supplementary weft under each row of tabby.

⑤ Add more columns and change colors.

⑥ The combination of colors and placement of columns together can make up a pattern when seen all together.

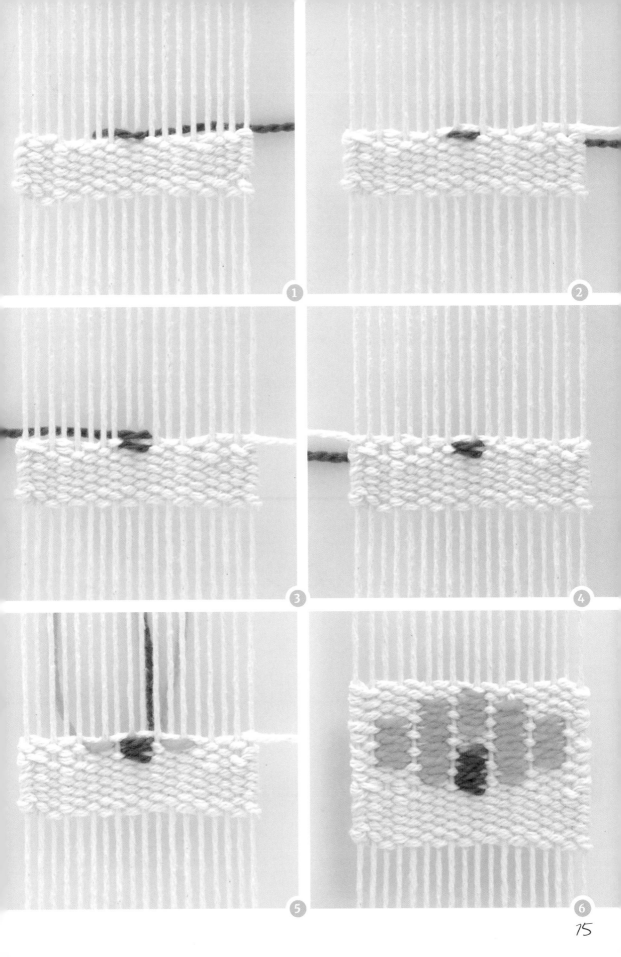

# Thrima

Level: Intermediate

Both thrima and sapma are supplementary weft techniques used in traditional Bhutanese techniques. Unlike overshot and krabbasnar, they use two tails of supplementary weft at a time. They also do not float in the back or even hang in the back until it is their time to come to the surface. Instead, the two tails always hang on the surface of the weave until they are needed between rows of plain tabby.

1. In Bhutan, *thrima* means "to coil," which is exactly what the supplementary weft does. For vertical columns of thrima, begin by hanging a length of yarn around two warp strings so that the tails hang down in the front.

2. Weave a row of plain tabby weave, using the foundational yarn.

3. Crisscross the tails in front of the two warp strings, then again crisscross them in the back so that they hang in the front again.

4. Continue alternating between rows of supplementary weft and background tabby, crisscrossing the supplementary weft after each tabby row. The coiling will resemble Xs on the front.

5. You can use this same technique to make larger-scale shapes such as diamonds and triangles by always crisscrossing in the front and then the back.

6. The double-soumak technique is also considered part of the thrima family because it uses two tails to coil around the warp strings. The vertical thrima and horizontal thrima are often used together to make patterns.

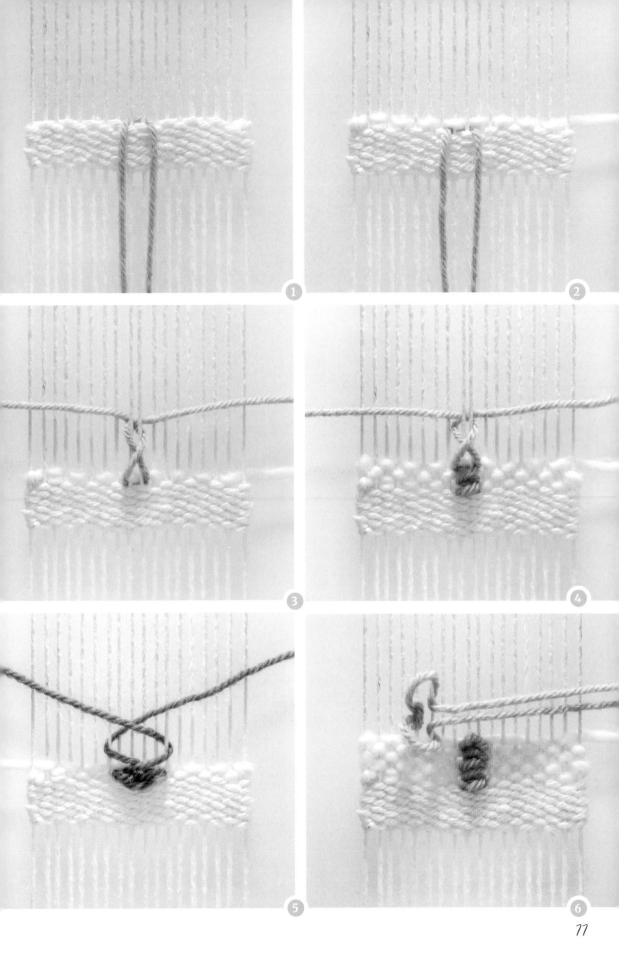

## Sapma

Level: Advanced | Projects: Delicate Details,
p. 114

Sapma is a supplementary weft technique that
is used in traditional Bhutanese weaving.
Unlike overshot and krabbasnar, it uses two
tails of supplementary weft at a time. They do
not float in the back or hang in the back until
it is their time to come to the surface. Instead,
the two tails always hang on the surface of the
weave until they are needed to cross between
rows of plain tabby.

1. It may help to sketch a sapma design
   before starting to help you stay on
   track. Begin by hanging a length of
   yarn on the first row of the pattern so
   that the tails hang down in the front.

2. Weave a row of plain tabby weave,
   using the foundational yarn, and then
   add a second row of sapma. As the two
   tails move among the warp, going over
   and under to create their pattern, they
   crisscross. It may help to do one side
   and then the other.

3. Each time the sapma begins a new row,
   each tail goes over the warp string it
   ended going under the last time. This
   creates a small border around the
   outside of the shape, which is charac-
   teristic of sapma.

4. Continue alternating between rows of
   supplementary weft and background
   tabby.

5. To finish a shape, tuck the two tails in
   the back.

6. Multiple small sapma shapes are often
   woven together, side by side in many
   different colors, for a larger, complex
   pattern.

## Pulled Threads

Pulled threads is a floating weaving technique that creates horizontal borders in delicate lacy
patterns. It is also known as gauze weave and cross weave. These weaving techniques can also be done
with thin, tightly woven fabric that has been removed from the loom in an embroidery method called
pulled thread. It is the only technique that intentionally moves your warp out of its parallel vertical
alignment. In this method you will twist the warp strings over and under each other in groups to
create patterns that are held tightly in place by a single weft yarn.

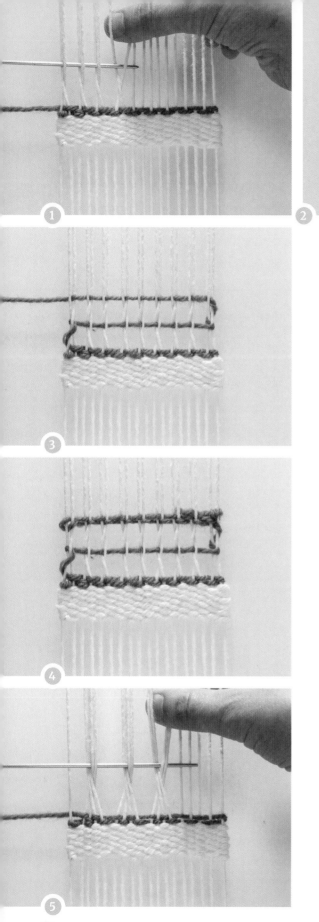

# Leno

Level: Intermediate

The most common leno lace twists groups of two warp strings around each other. Use a smooth, strong length of yarn that is 1.5 times the width of your tapestry to twist the warp strings.

① Twist your warp strings in pairs of two by pulling the far warp string over the top of the near warp strings and over.

② Use your needle to guide the weft through the twists to hold them in place.

③ Move on to the next row and twist the warp strings back.

④ When you are done with the single-twist lace leno, continue weaving tabby as normal to get your warp strings back in place.

⑤ This method can be done with larger groups of warp strings, such as four. Instead of pulling one warp string over another, pull two warp strings over two others, etc. There are also more-complex leno twists involving four to six warp strings.

# Brooks Bouquet

Level: Intermediate | Projects: Framed
Loom, p. 104

Brooks bouquet is another form of leno lace
that pulls groups of warps together and ties
them with the single weft row. It creates large,
open spaces in a lacy border.

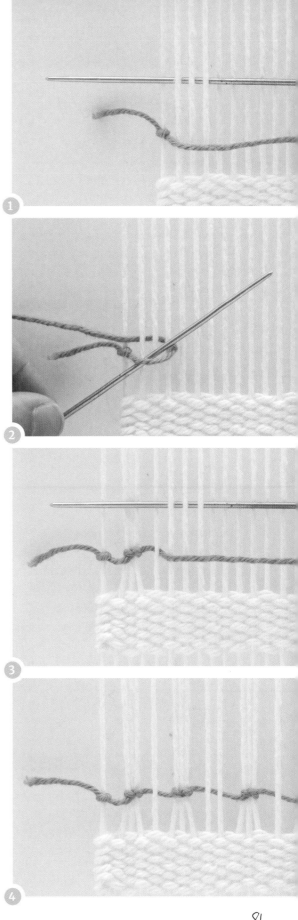

1. Begin by wrapping your weft around
   the front of a bundle of warp strings
   and then to the back.

2. When you come around to the front
   again, tie a knot by guiding the weft up
   through the loop, in front of the warp
   strings. Some weavers use a simple
   wrap instead of a knot, but knotting
   helps the weft tightly hold your
   bundles together.

3. Guide the weft under the next warp
   string and then around the front of the
   next bundle, to the back.

4. Continue tying knots around each
   bundle.

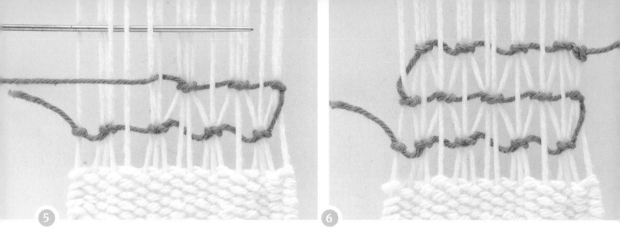

5　To create patterns, when you move on to the next row, tie together warp strings from different bundles so that the warp crisscrosses between the bundles.

6　This technique will pull your warp tighter than usual. If you do not have an adjustable loom, warp your loom looser than usual or weave only a small amount of Brooks bouquets so that the warp isn't too tight to continue weaving.

## Spanish Lace

Level: Intermediate

Spanish lace uses a regular tabby weave across smaller sections of warp strings at a time. Although the warps do not twist around each other, they are pulled out of their even alignment as each section is intentionally pulled tight to emphasize the distinct shapes. The weft for your Spanish lace should be a thick, smooth cord to distinguish the pattern.

Decide how many sections of Spanish lace you want to create. Each section should be the same size, so divide your number of total warp strings into sections that are six to twelve warp strings wide each.

1　Begin by passing your cord through the warp strings in the first section using a plain tabby technique.

2　When you reach the end, turn around and pass it back through the same number of warp strings.

3　When you reach the end, turn the cord around and make one final pass through the same number of warp strings, so that you have three stacked rows in the same section. As you are weaving, pull your rows tight to emphasize the shape.

4　Use your continuous yarn to move on to the next section, where you stack three more rows across the same number of warp strings.

# Waffle Weave

Level: Advanced | **Projects: Fringed Patterns, p. 124**

Waffle weave is created from a varying mix of floating wefts and warps. When removed from the loom they contract into high and low textures that resemble the shape of a waffle! You can make your waffle squares as big or small as you want simply by adding on to the rows on the edge before reflecting them and working back toward the center.

1. Use the pattern included to create a waffle weave that has floats seven warp strings across. This is a good number before the floats become too long and drape.

2. When you turn around, do your best to follow the edge of the pattern, but keep in mind that your selvedge (last warp string on either side) is flexible to working outside the pattern so that your weft always loops around it.

3. As your weft floats across one side, the warp is floating perpendicular on the other side. (If your warp floats from left to right on the top, the warp is floating from top to bottom on the bottom.) Use one color for the warp and one for the weft for a checkerboard effect, or the same color for both for a seamless design.

4. You should still bubble each row to keep your edges straight.

5. When you get to the center, reflect the pattern sequence to taper off your waffle weave to a point again, and then repeat.

## Advanced Tip

If you want square waffles, your warp should be either the same width apart as your weft, or even better yet, the same yarn completely. If your warp is too far apart or too thin compared to your weft, you will get oblong waffles.

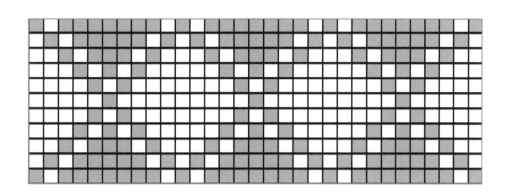

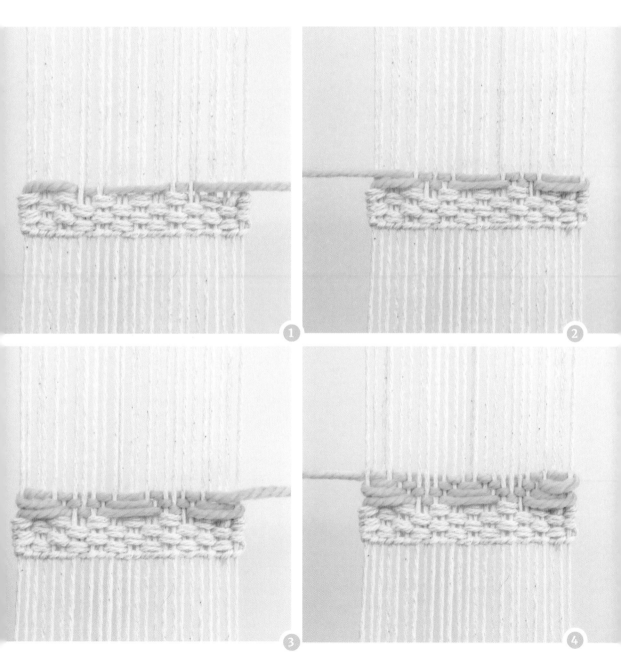

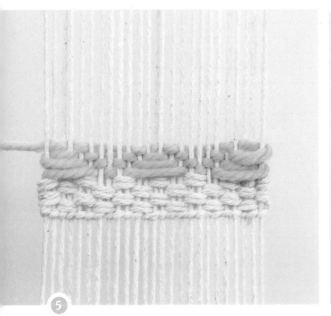

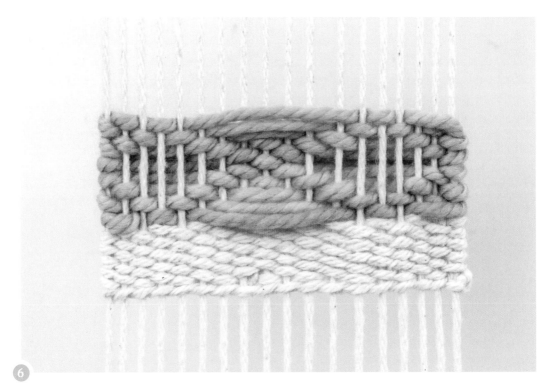

When you remove your waffle weave from the loom the floats will contract, making the center of your floats on either side extra high on each side, and your diamonds will turn into squares, with the end points becoming the center. It's like magic!

# Krokbragd

Level: Advanced | Projects: Fringed
Patterns, p. 124

Krokbragd is a time-consuming weft-faced
weave, which means no warp shows through.
The front of your tapestry will look similar to
pixelated designs, while the back is covered by
short floats. It uses three rows, packed tightly
together to produce one row. This allows you to
create intricate designs within a small space.

*(Step-by-step pictures on following page)*

(Step-by-step pictures on following page)

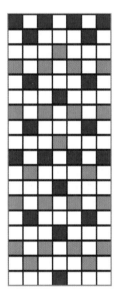

① Use the pattern included to create a
flower pattern using two different
colors. The pattern may not look like
your finished product, which is a little
confusing, but that's because three
rows of weft will be beaten down to create one row, just like a puzzle! The first
row will cover every fourth warp string,
floating behind three warp strings in
between.

② The second row will also cover every
warp string, floating behind three warp
strings in between. The warp string that
the second row covers will be the
middle of the three warp strings that
the first row floats behind.

③ The third row will cover every other
warp string, just like a regular tabby
technique. When these three rows are
beaten down, together they will cover
all the warp strings in a single row.

## Advanced Tip

All of your yarns should be about the same
thickness. If you need to, you can double up
a thinner yarn to match the thickness of the
others. The space between your rows
should be the same as the thickness of your
yarns for an even 1:1 ratio for proportional
designs. (Warp strings that are too far apart
or too close together will stretch your
design longways or topways.)

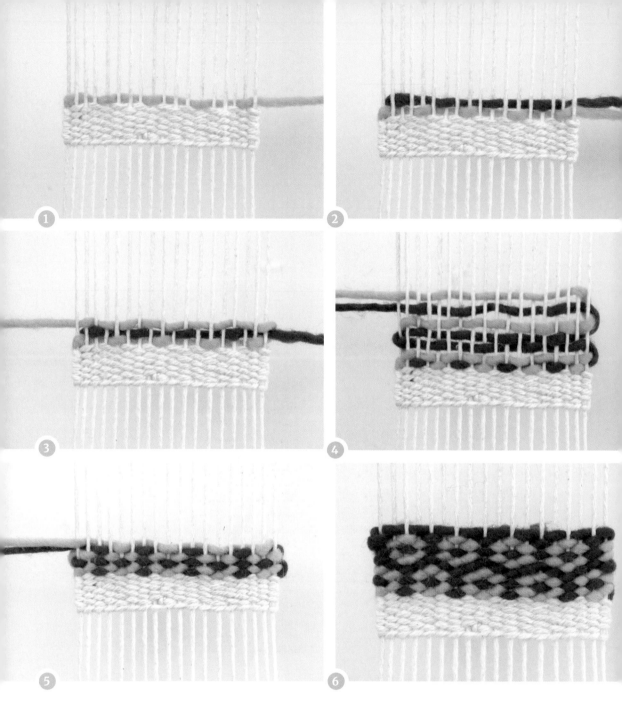

4 Repeat the sequence of the three rows: the first two rows covering opposites of every fourth warp string and the third row covering the rest of the warp strings that the first two rows missed.

5 Beat the rows down to see the pattern emerge.

6 The sequence is the same for all krokbragd weaving, but by switching colors you can create all kinds of patterns.

# Deflected Double Weave

Level: Advanced | Projects: Fringed
Patterns, p. 124

This technique requires your warp to be the same yarn and colors as your weft. It plays off the intersection between the warp versus weft to create different patterns. It is always done with stripes, so your warp will either need to be striped one after the other, or in pairs, or more. Single stripes (one color after the other) will use a pick and pick weaving method. The wider your stripes, the easier it will be to notice the pattern.

## Advanced Tip

Use a piece of paper within the shed of your warp to help you visualize what colors your weft is weaving under and what colors will be shown in the row.

## Single Stripes

1. Use the pattern included to create a subtle diamond shape in the center of your sample, using single stripes. Begin by warping your loom with single stripes. Tie the same two colors together and begin using a pick and pick method to weave them in.

2. When you get to the point of the diamond, float one color over both of the warp string colors. The color that is shown on front will be the color that shows up in the pattern, so by floating, you hide the opposite color behind the weft.

3. Use a piece of paper to help you visualize. Here, on the edges the pattern continues the pick and pick sequence, but in the center, where the diamond is taking place, the opposite pick and pick sequence is happening so that only one color is showing. The floats on either side allow the row to switch to an opposite pick and pick.

4. Again, the opposite pick and pick within the center creates a diamond shape.

5. Continue following the pattern and sequence to know when to switch the pick and pick.

6. You can see when you are done that on a single-stripe deflected double weave, a pick and pick technique usually creates vertical stripes, but when you switch it creates horizontal stripes, for a subtle pattern within the weave.

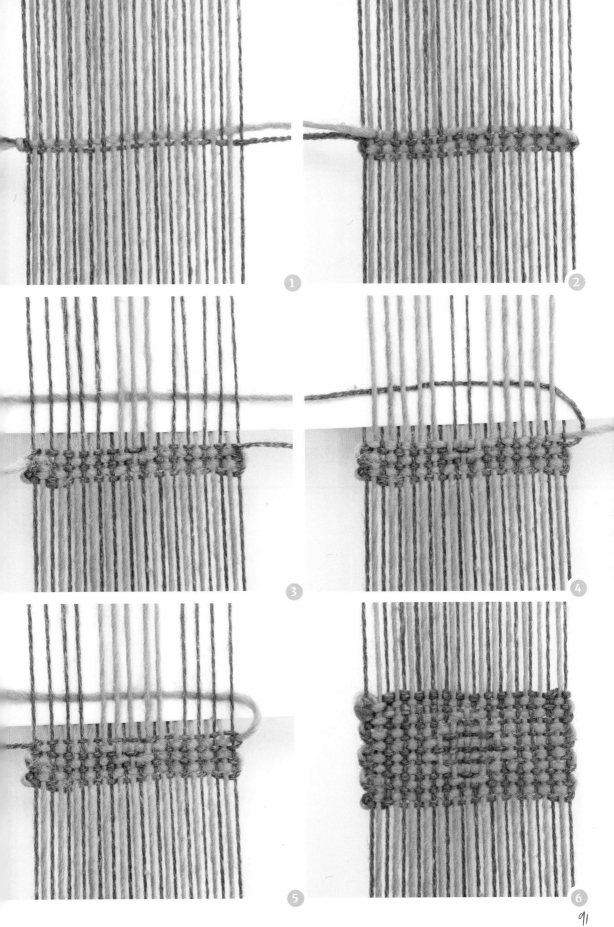

# Double Stripes

You can use the same method with double stripes, where there are pairs of each color on the warp and weft. This method is also used for stripes that have three or more colors. The same warp and weft colors should always weave within each other and always float over or under the opposite color. Whether they float over the top or underneath determines the pattern.

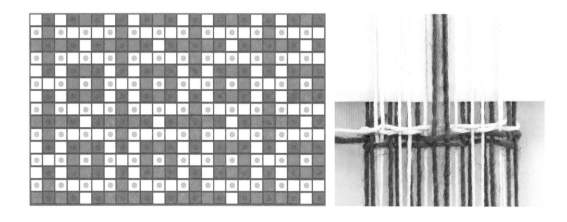

The front of the deflected double weave will be reflected on the backside to create an opposite design.

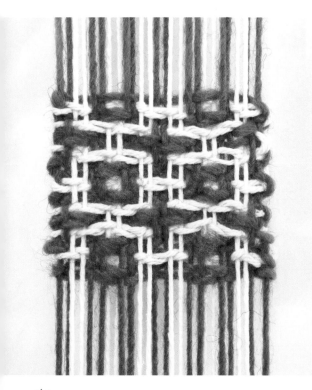

# Knit Weave

Level: Advanced | **Projects:** Fringed Patterns, p. 124

This technique appears to defy gravity by allowing plaits to move vertically along your warp. It looks similar to a soumak moving across your warp instead of your weft.

1. The first row of knit weave needs a row of twining to loop around to secure it to your warp. Begin with a row of twining around pairs of warp string.

2. Use a needle to guide your yarn around up through a twining loop, around the back of a pair of warp strings, and then down through a twining loop before moving on to the next pair.

3. Complete an entire row. You can space out your warp strings or loop around two to four at once, but like rya, you need at least two warp strings exiting out the top of each loop.

4. Use your needle to guide your yarn from the back, up through the center of the pair of warp strings and the loop of yarn.

5. Now guide the needle around from front to back and down through the center of the pair of warp strings and loop of yarn. You will notice this is the same movement as an upside-down rya knot.

6. Move on to the next loop, repeating the same movement by going up through the center, around the back, down through the center, and moving on.

7. As you continue, your rows will grow upward, mimicking a soumak or knit technique.

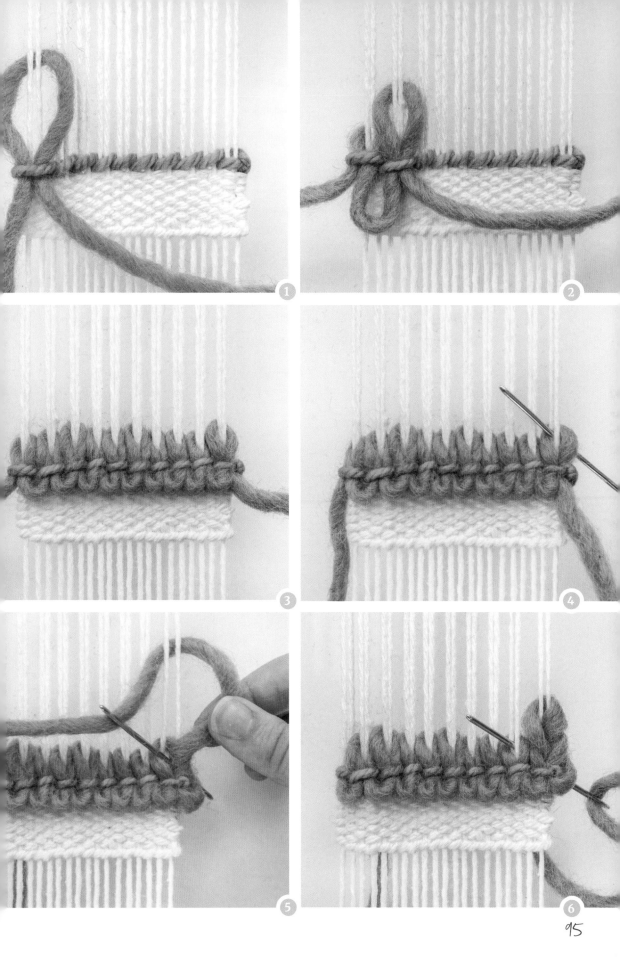

# Mawhitiwhiti

Level: Advanced | Projects: Mawhitiwhiti Off-Loom, p. 118

Mawhitiwhiti is a New Zealand Maori weaving technique. This is unlike any other weaving technique in the book because it is actually done without a loom. It uses double twining rows to anchor each warp string. Without a loom keeping the warp strings tight and secure, it allows them to be the star of the show as they travel across the tapestry, creating patterns while the twining is the supporting element.

## Advanced Tip

Unlike most other weaving techniques, your warp should be thicker than your weft. Since the warp will be moving, it will lose a bit of length with each row, and you won't want to knot more on without messing up the aesthetics of the piece, so plan accordingly and budget in extra length, depending on the design.

1. Knot your warp onto a dowel or pin it into foamcore board so that it is secure on top, but loose on bottom. Choose a thinner yarn to use for the double twining weft rows. Fold two lengths in half around the first warp string so that there are two on top and two on bottom.

2. For double twining, the bottom two pieces of yarn come up between the center of the top two pieces of yarn.

3. Then the top pieces go underneath the next warp string, becoming the new bottom pieces of yarn and continuing the sequence. Bottom comes up between the center of the top, and top goes under the next warp string to become the new bottom, which comes up between the center of the top.

4. Continue the sequence across the width of the warp strings. When you reach the end, go back and walk your fingers across each warp string, making sure they are evenly spaced. Tie a knot with the twining wefts on the end.

5. Before you begin the next row of double twining, cross any warp strings that you want to move as part of the pattern. Then add another row of double twining to keep them in place.

6. There are many patterns you can create by simply moving the warp strings before each double twining row. You can also play with the pattern by pushing the twining rows closer or farther away from each other, lengthening or shortening the distance for each warp string to move.

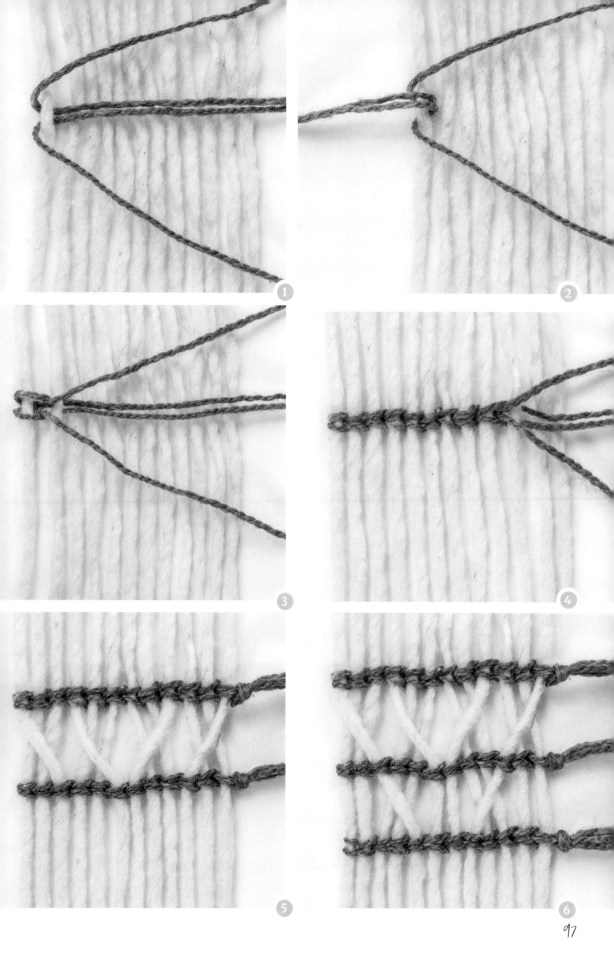

## Ready to put your new skills to work?

In this section you will find a few tapestry designs to follow, using the techniques in previous parts of the book. You can follow along to make each one with the instructions, or mix and match the techniques to make something up yourself. The yarn you use will be different than my own collection, so feel free to play along by choosing a weight similar to what I am using, or experiment with something much different.

Each design shows its level of difficulty and is labeled with which techniques were used. There are some references to basic techniques (which are taught in my book *Welcome to Weaving*), but all of the more-advanced techniques shared in this book show page numbers so you can go back to review them.

# Section 4
# THE TAPESTRIES

*TECHNIQUES*

# The
# Textural Sampler
## Tapestry

Textural techniques take a tapestry from 2-D to 3-D. This piece will help you practice some of the most textural techniques along with a large section of plain tabby weave. Try using materials that are all in the same color family for a design that looks concise, even with the large number of techniques.

*Tips*    Tabby rows and twining rows will help pack down textural techniques and keep your warp strings nice and straight, especially with thick materials.

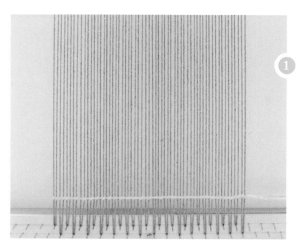

**1** Decide how wide you want your tapestry to be, warp your loom, and add a twining header row.

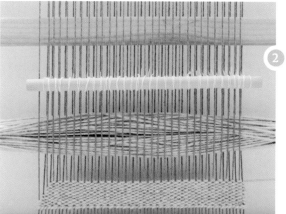

**2** Begin with a large, triangular area of plain tabby weave. If you use the same yarn for this area, it is helpful to use a shuttle stick, pick-up stick, and heddle together so that you can weave faster with very few interruptions. Don't forget bubbling and beating so that the sides stay straight!

7. Roving also adds great texture when used as organic loops. Add it as tabby and then gently pull out random bumps between warp strings with your fingers. After each row, add a single twining or tabby row to keep the tapestry from bulging from the loose technique.

8. Small, uncut bundles of rya knots add lots of texture. Wrap each bundle around two warp strings and add a few rows of tabby after each rya row to pack it in place.

9. One of my favorite ways to finish off a tapestry is with extra-thick fringe. Cut two lengths per warp string for each row and wrap bundles of 12 around six warp strings at once as rya for this effect. Don't forget to add a few rows of tabby after each rya row to pack it in place.

10. Finish the tapestry design with the hem stitch at the bottom.

11. Turn the tapestry around and make sure all the tails are tucked in and trimmed. Then cut the tapestry off the loom.

12. Use the overhand knot on each warp loop at the top of the tapestry.

13. Turn the tapestry over and sew on the rod.

3. The large, triangular tabby area will angle from one corner of the tapestry, tapering off at the end.

4. Now for the texture. Using an extra-thick yarn, add an inverse triangle of tabby. Even though it is also the plain tabby weave, the extra-chunky yarn will add lots of texture and shape.

5. Use a pencil roving to add a few rows of pile weave. A knitting needle is a great tool to keep the loops symmetrical. After each row of loops, don't forget to add a full pass (two rows) of twining to hold them tightly in place.

6. Use a length of unspun roving for a thick braid with the soumak technique. Tuck the edges underneath.

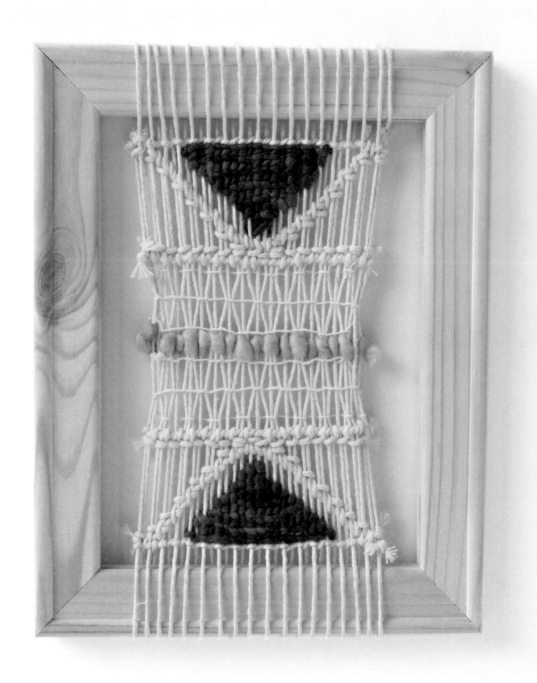

*TECHNIQUES*

# The
# Framed Loom
## Tapestry

This tapestry uses a wooden frame as the loom and to display the finished piece. The tapestry is never removed from the loom, so there is little work to do at the end. Because the frame keeps the warp strings taut, and the tapestry is never cut off the loom, you can experiment with techniques in a delicate, open format without adding supporting rows to give the tapestry structure on its own.

*Tips* Use a strong cotton twine for most of the techniques in this tapestry for extra durability.

1  Use a wooden frame from a canvas stretcher or picture frame. The size of the frame will dictate the size of the finished piece.

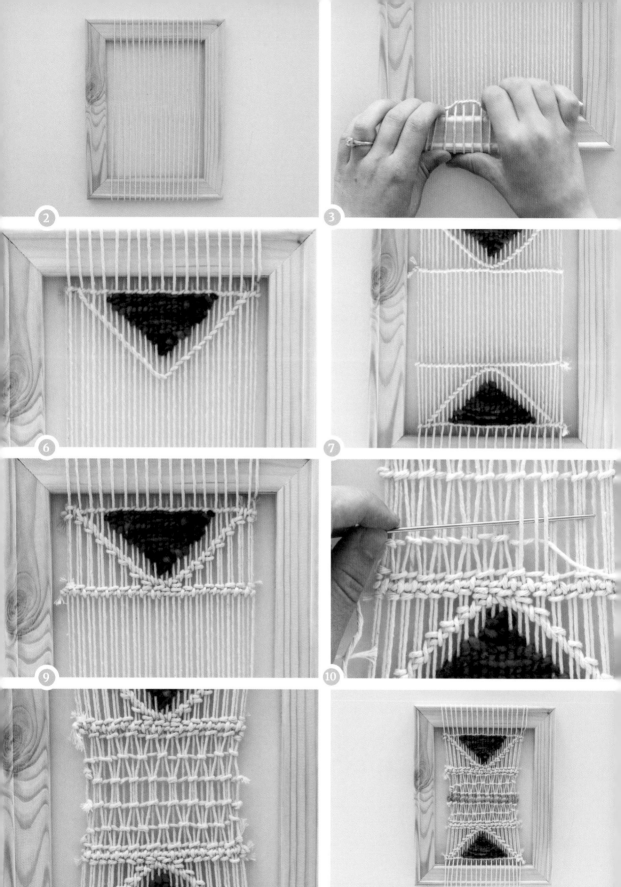

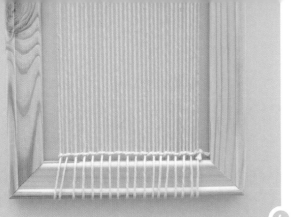

6. Add another twining row on both sides of the tapestry. Beat them down so that both create a triangle shape with space between the twining and the Egyptian knot shape.

7. Add another twining row on both sides of the tapestry, straight across the top of the twining triangle.

8. Add a hem stitch above the twining triangle and below the twining row.

9. Even though the twining row will stay in place on its own because the warp strings are held taut on the loom, the hem stitch will pull two warp strings closer together within these shapes, for some design interest.

10. Add a few rows of Brooks bouquet. You can tie each bouquet with a knot for tight bundles or simply loop the weft for a looser bundle.

11. The Brooks bouquet will be in bundles of two to three and alternate with each row for a lattice effect.

12. Add a final row of Egyptian knot in the center of the design. You don't have to cut the tapestry off the loom or sew it onto a rod, so you are done!

2. Tie a knot at the top of the frame and warp the loom, using a figure-eight pattern by wrapping from the front to the back each time you move from top to bottom. This will make it easier for the warp strings to be straight in the middle.

3. Create a twining header on the top and bottom of the loom. Use a comb or your fingers to pull a row to either side, as close to the edge as you can.

4. Now the warp strings in the middle are on the same plane, just like on a regular loom with nails.

5. Use Egyptian knot (backwards soumak) to create triangles on either side of the tapestry.

# General Circular-Weaving Tips

Weaving on a circular loom is very similar to weaving on a regular frame loom, but there are some important differences to remember.

**1** Do not begin with a twining header. There is no need for a twining header because you will begin at the center of your tapestry, so you don't have to worry about rows shifting when the weave is removed from the loom.

**2** Begin with a thin yarn. At the center of your loom the warp strings will be extra close together, so only a thin yarn will fit. To start weaving, simply tie a knot on one of the center warp strings and begin a regular tabby weave!

**3** Spiral for continuous rows. When you complete a row, simply continue weaving for continuous rows. The spiral works because you have an odd number of warp strings, so when your weft ends a row by going under a warp string, it will automatically be able to go over the next warp string to create the next row.

**4** Interlock for rows that turn around. If you decide you don't want your rows to continue in a straight spiral, you can work upward just as you would on a frame loom by hooking your weft around a warp string and turning it back around to stack the next row. If you do this, always remember to interlock your rows when they stack next to each other, whether they are different colors or different materials. As the warp strings get farther from the center they get farther apart, so gaps are very noticeable if they are not interlocked.

**5** Try all weaving techniques. Twill, soumak, loops, rya, even Spanish lace—all are fair game for circular weaving, so have fun experimenting.

*Tips*   Just as you began with a thin yarn at the center of your tapestry, thicker yarns work best toward the outside of your circular weave. The warp gets farther apart, leaving ample room to weave your thick materials through for a prominent outer border.

# Teneriffe Lace

Another technique to use on circular looms is called Teneriffe lace. Teneriffe lace weaving is a traditional technique from France that creates lacy medallions. You do not interlock your rows but instead embrace the spaces that happen as your warp strings are pulled toward your weft rows. It is also common in Teneriffe lace to leave parts of your warp unwoven to create patterns, and to use pulled threads.

Teneriffe lace weaving is a separate craft of its own. The patterns can be very complex and traditional, and the end result is similar to a lace doily. Teneriffe lace should be woven with cotton, traditionally in the same unbleached color as the warp strings. No roving or extra colors are included. Of course, you can take inspiration from Teneriffe lace weaving to add a touch to your circular weaving here or there with whatever materials you choose.

One easy Teneriffe lace pattern resembles a flower blooming from the center of your circular tapestry. Begin by warping your hoop so that the number of warp strings is divisible by the number of petals you want in your flower, whether it's four, five, six, or seven. Begin weaving each section separately without interlocking the edges of your rows and pulling your wefts tightly so that the petals are distinguished as separate. As you get farther away from the center of the tapestry, begin weaving fewer and fewer rows to create the tip of each petal.

*TECHNIQUES*

Looped Rya, p. 49 | Tabby, p. 22

# The
# Free-Form Hoop
# Tapestry

Do you want the circular tapestry with a horizontal weft? If you don't want your weft rows to spiral out from the center, you can use your hoop the same way you would weave with a frame loom.

*Tips* Your warp might be farther apart than on a regular loom, so double up thinner yarns or use thicker yarns to cover space more easily.

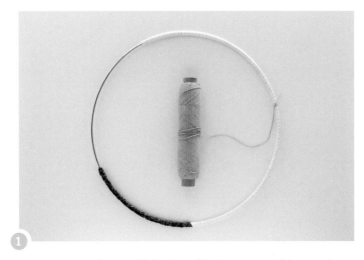

1. Wrap your hoop with leather, fabric, yarn, or ribbon so that your warp strings won't slip. Tie your first warp string at the 2:30 position on the hoop. Because your warp strings will lie parallel across the hoop instead of converging in the center, your warp strings will be different lengths. They will be longer in the center and shorter on the side. This first warp string will be at the side of your hoop and thus will be the shortest warp string.

2 Pull your warp string down straight, about 2–3", depending on the size of your hoop. Wrap it from the front of the hoop to the back, but as you come back up, guide your string through the loop, between the warp and the small side of the hoop.

3 Instead of immediately going back up to the top of your hoop, guide your string ½" along the bottom front of the hoop and then wrap it back around to the back, coming up underneath the connecting string, parallel to your hoop. It helps to wrap your warp strings loosely around to the back of the hoop so that you can guide your large cone of yarn through, underneath the connecting strings. Then make sure to tighten the loop after each pass for a durable warp.

4 When your second warp string is tied to the bottom of the hoop, pull it straight up to its place at the top and wrap it around from the front to the back and then up between the first and second warp string before guiding it over ½", parallel to the hoop.

5 Continue wrapping your string from top to bottom, over, bottom to top,

over, top to bottom, etc., until you have warped the chosen amount of space for your hoop.

6 On the last warp string, tie a knot.

7 Now that your hoop is vertically warped, you can begin weaving in the regular way by creating horizontal wefts. Add some rya on the bottom and fill it in with soumak or tabby. You do not need to create a twining header or end with a hem stitch, because your weave will not be removed from the loom.

8 As you are weaving, pay attention to the shape of the loom. Keep in mind that your tabby weft rows will need to be shorter at the bottom of your circular loom and wider in the middle so that they hug the boundary of the circle.

9 Continue adding rows of tabby and soumak. Because your warp strings will be a bit farther apart, it is important to dovetail your rows so that there are no big gaps between the warp strings.

## TECHNIQUES

Pile Weave, p. 43 | Krabbasnar, p. 74 | Twining Patterns, p. 62 | Sapma, p. 78 |
Twisted Floaters, p. 45 | Finishing without Fringe, p. 36

# The
# Delicate Details
## Tapestry

Some of the more advanced techniques take a lot of time and concentration, so this smaller, framed tapestry is the perfect size for focusing on them!

*Tips* Choose a similar weight for all the yarns used in this tapestry, so that the techniques work together the best. One solid color yarn will work as the foundational tabby weave within all the techniques.

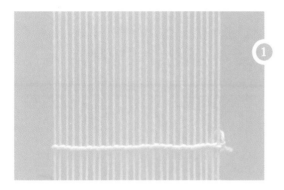

**1** Decide how wide you want your tapestry, warp your loom, and add a twining header row.

**2** Create a triangle from the pile weave technique. After each pile weave row, add a full pass (two rows) of tabby to lock it in place.

**3** Use a bundle of three yarns or a loosely spun rope to add more texture and detail to the pile weave triangle.

4. Add a few rows of krabbasnar. Each column is made with a single length of yarn. The yarn hangs in the back until each single row of tabby, after which each yarn will flip over two warp strings to hang in the back again, waiting for the next row of tabby.

5. The krabbasnar columns can begin and end at different tabby rows to mimic the shape of the pile weave triangle.

6. Use two different colors of yarn to create a twining row. At the center of each row, switch the direction of the twining from overtwining to undertwining. After five to six rows, reverse the overtwining and undertwining to create a radiating diamond pattern.

7. Tuck the tails of both yarns from the twining pattern underneath. Twining patterns take a lot of concentration and practice. Don't give up! The patterns may be difficult to notice until the end, so make it easy on yourself and use two contrasting-colored yarns. Add a quick row of double soumak before the next technique.

8. Create a small triangle of krabbasnar and then two chevrons of sapma. Each shape is made with two tails. The yarn hangs in front until each single row of tabby, after which each yarn crosses in front of the warp strings to hang in the front again, waiting for the next row of tabby.

   It helps to use grid paper to draw a pattern for your sapma beforehand.

9. Create rows of twisted floaters, followed by a few rows of tabby to hold them in place.

10. Turn the weave around and make sure all the tails are tucked in and ends are trimmed. Then remove it from the loom. Go through and tuck each extra warp string down through a few rows of tabby, and trim the tails.

11. Sew the finished tapestry onto a piece of card stock and frame it to show off the details of your delicate piece!

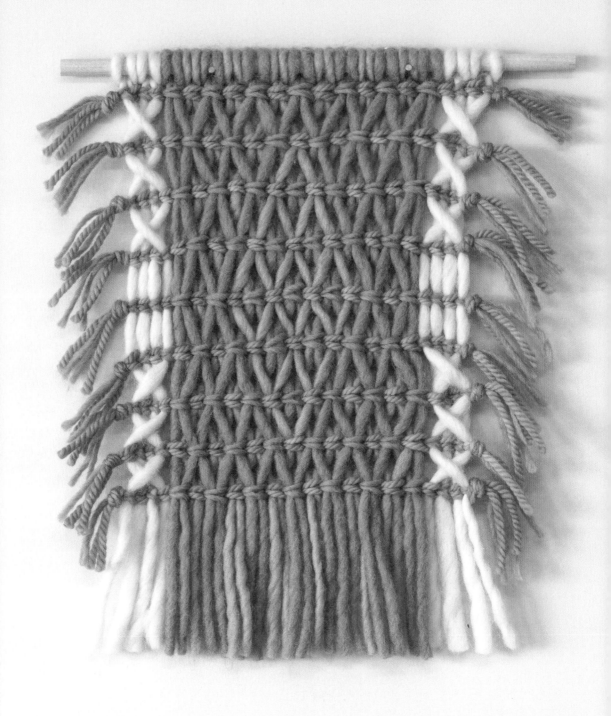

TECHNIQUES

Mawhitiwhiti, p. 96

# The Mawhitiwhiti Off-Loom Tapestry

This tapestry is woven without a loom, using the basic techniques of Mawhitiwhiti in a creative way to create shapes on the surface.

*Tips*

You will need three colors of chunky yarn for your warp and two colors of thinner yarn for your weft. Make sure the thinner yarn matches two of the colors of chunky yarn as closely as possible so that they blend into the pattern instead of standing out.

Decide how wide you want your tapestry. Fold your warp in half and use a reverse larkshead knot to attach it to your dowel. I am using lengths of yarn that are each about 4 feet long, folded in half so that once they are knotted on the dowel they are each about 2 feet long. As you are working your warp will lose length. Use pins to secure your dowel onto foamcore, or hang it on a wall to keep it from slipping around.

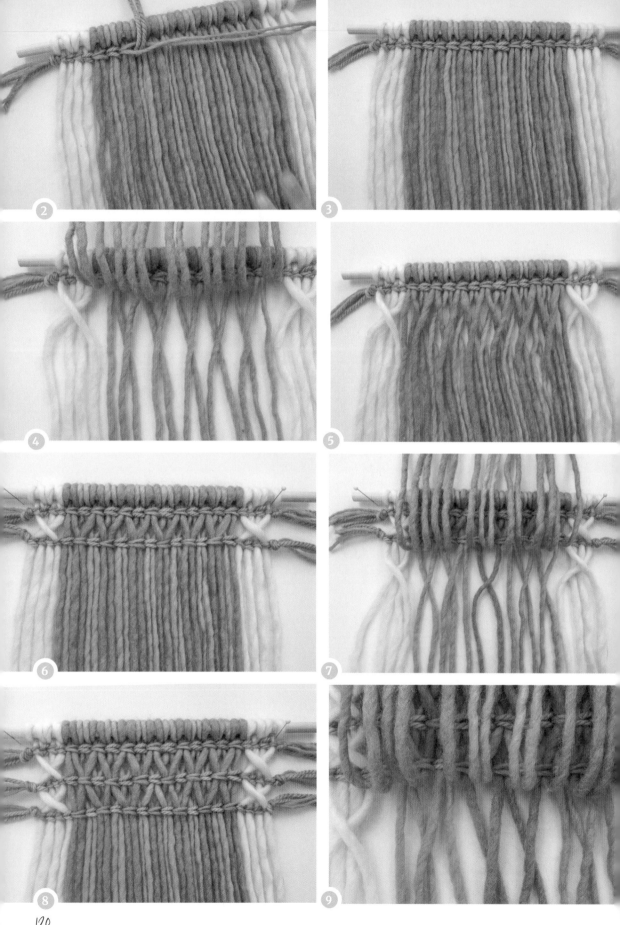

2 Tie four 20" strands of thin weft together with a 2" tail. Two should match the color of one of your center warp colors, and the other two should match the color of the other center warp color. Use a double twining technique across the width of the top of your warp. Twine around one warp strand for each of the outside columns and around two warp strings at once for the main pattern section.

3 Make sure that the weft colors on top match up with the warp colors as you are twining. Tie a knot on the end of the weft strands with a 2" tail.

4 Now we will begin creating patterns with the warp strings. Follow the pattern included. An easy way to keep control of the pattern is to lift all the strands that you want to be shown on the front of the row. Warp strands that lie on the top will be shown on the front of the tapestry. For the first row, lift all of one color and cross the colors that remain, excluding the two outside strands. You can also cross the two outside strands on the outside columns.

5 Now lower all the warp strands that you want to show up on the front, and cross them between the bottom strands, excluding the two outside strands.

6 Use a row of double twining across the width of your warp, securing the bottom layer of crossed warps and the top layer of crossed warps so that each color of twining matches up with the same color of warp.

7 Now move on to the next row of patterns with warp strings. Lift all the strands that you want to be shown on the front of the row, and cross the ones that remain, excluding the ends. Since we are beginning a diamond shape, there will be a mix of both colors of warp strings in the center. As the diamond gets bigger you will add more warp strands from underneath to the top and vice versa.

8 Lay all of the top warp strands and cross them on top of the bottom ones and then add a double twining row to secure two layers of crossed warps, making sure each color of twining matches up with the same color of warp.

9 Move on to the next row of patterns with warp strings. Lift all the strands that you want to be shown on the front, and cross the ones that are left, excluding any ends. There will be a mix of both colors of warp strings to create more of the diamond shape.

⑩ Lay all the top warp strands and cross them on top of the bottom ones, then add a double twining row to secure two layers of crossed warps, making sure each color of twining matches up with the same color of warp.

⑪ Move on to the next row of patterns with warp strings, following the same steps as before.

⑫ Add a row of double twining.

⑬ This is the center of your diamond shape, so reflect the pattern from the first four rows to complete the bottom of the diamond shape and finish the tapestry. When you are done, simply trim the bottom and the strands on either side to be straight and even.

# Off-Loom Twining Technique

Twining without a loom is a little more difficult because your warp strings aren't held in place. Here's how to make sure your twining rows are nice and tight.

1. Move across the row, twining around one to two strands, depending on what the pattern calls for. Your row will be loose and uneven, but don't worry—just get the right colors on top of the right warp strands, and we will fix tension later.

2. Now tighten the row by holding on to pieces of your twining row and gently pulling the warp strands from one end to the other to tighten the twining around them. When they are tight, knot the end of the twining-row strands.

3. Grab each pair of warp strings and gently push the twining row around them up into place so that it is parallel to the previous twining rows.

## TECHNIQUES

Wrapped Top, p. 38 | Knit Weave, p. 93 | Krokbragd, p. 87 |
Waffle Weave, p. 84 | Deflected Double Weave, p. 89

# The
# Fringed Patterns
## Tapestry

This tapestry is the perfect way to practice the advanced pattern techniques. Choose yarns in the same color family to keep the theme consistent as you move from one pattern to the next.

Tips — Patterns are easiest to start and stop on a flat line, so while you are practicing, keep your patterns separated into strips. You can get creative by separating them with curves or angles once you've mastered them.

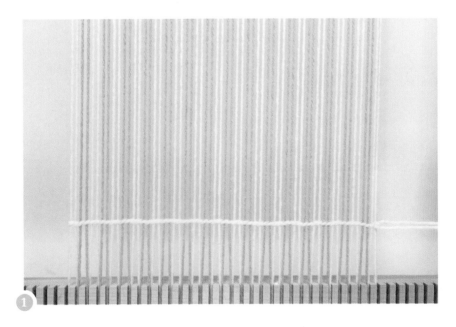

Decide how wide you want your tapestry, warp your loom, and add a twining header row. Plan ahead for the deflected double weave pattern at the bottom and warp your loom with double stripes in your preferred colors.

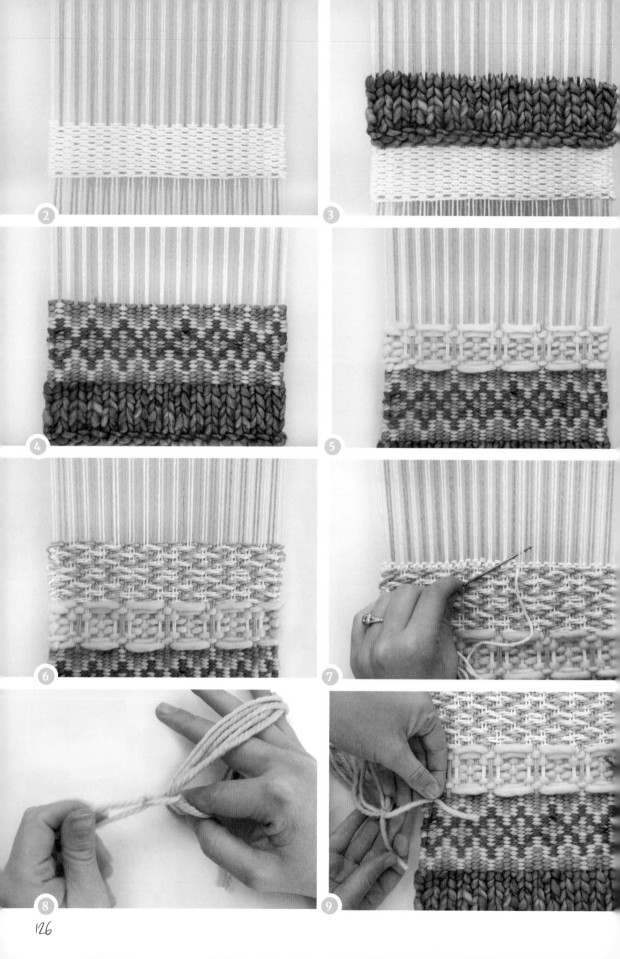

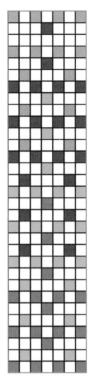

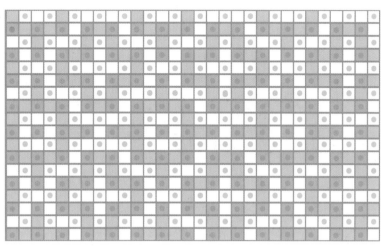

2. Add a section of tabby (you can double it up to move on faster). This top part will be wrapped around your dowel to hang your tapestry from, so make sure it is the right length to fit.

3. Add five to six rows of knit weave, beginning with a row of twining in the same color to anchor the technique.

4. Time to practice some krokbragd! Follow the pattern included to create this section. It uses four different colors of yarns. You can go over two warp strings at a time, depending on how close together they are. Extend or subtract the pattern, depending on how many warp strings you have. The warp will be completely covered.

5. Now add a single boxed row of waffle weave. This will take nine rows of yarn to complete and can be extended or subtracted, depending on how many warp strings you have. You can go over two warp strings at a time, depending on how close together they are.

6. Use the same yarns as your warp to complete a section of deflected double weave. Follow the pattern included to create this section by weaving stripes of the two colors, two at a time. Extend or subtract the pattern, depending on how many warp strings you have.

7. Finish your tapestry with a row of hem stitch.

8. If you want to add tassels to the sides and bottom of your tapestry, use your fingers to create bundles of five strands, tie them in the center with the same yarn, and trim the ends.

9. Use a needle to guide one tail from the tassels along the perimeter of your tapestry, 1" to 2" apart, and knot them on. You can use two different colors of tassels for a striped effect.

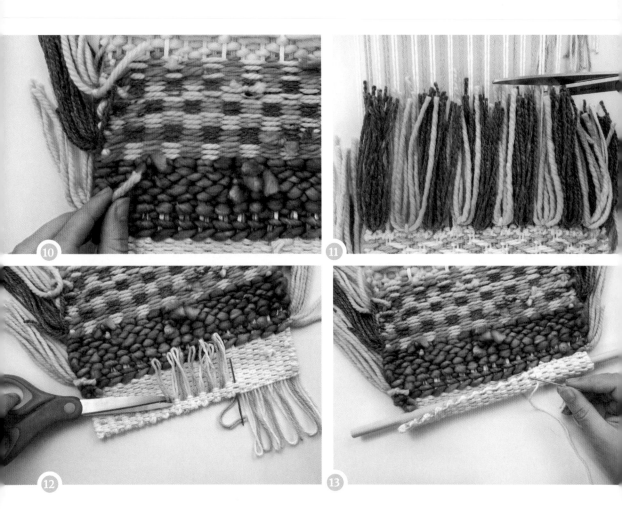

⑩ This is a view of the backside of your tapestry. The deflected double weave and waffle weave should look like reflections of the frontside, while the knit weave and krokbragd look completely different. Tuck any tails and clean up the back.

⑪ Cut the bottom of your tapestry off the loom.

⑫ Tuck the warp strings at the top of your tapestry over the twining row and into a few rows of weft before snipping the tails.

⑬ Wrap your top tabby section around your dowel and sew it on to secure it, and then your tapestry is ready to hang up and enjoy!

Section 5
THE PROJECTS

# Other Ways to Use Weaving

The advanced techniques in this book add a new level of tools for you to consider when approaching a project. Don't stop there! Now that you have an elevated knowledge of different ways to make your weaving designs stand out, you are ready to take on some projects beyond the basic tapestry or pillow. Think of your weaving as a piece of flexible fabric—it can be used as such to create anything you can imagine, from upholstery to bags, rugs, and even clothing. You may need to get your hands dirty and build a bigger loom if you have a big project in mind (see page 17), but don't let that limit your ideas!

The projects in this section of the book are meant to be used as ideas to jump-start your own creativity. The specifics given for each woven panel in these projects are less detailed than the instructions for techniques or tapestries from earlier in the book. This is because I don't want you to get caught up in questions like "exactly how many rows" and "exactly what kind of yarn" . . . I want you to incorporate your own materials and designs. The instructions in this project section focus mostly on how to take everything you have learned and transform it into something you can use and showcase in a new way. What will you think of?

# Zipper Pouch

Put your weaving skills to work by creating this eye-catching zippered pouch. It's the perfect accessory to carry around. If you already know how to sew, this project is easy, but if you don't, just practice a bit before you begin sewing your tapestry up. This piece can be created with any techniques you want to use, but if you want a textural fringe or soumak, be mindful of the materials and where you place them within the weaving so that the pouch will be functional.

You will need a sewing machine (you can sew this project by hand, but a sewing machine makes steps 3, 4, and 5 much easier), a 9" nonseparating zipper, a tapestry, and a lining fabric.

1. Complete your tapestry. It is easiest if the top and bottom are bordered with about 1" of tightly woven, thin tabby rows so that you can sew through them easily. A twining header should be at the top and bottom instead of a hem stitch, for a smoother finish. Cut your tapestry off the loom and tuck the ends of the warp strings into the backside before trimming them.

2. Cut a piece of lining 1" larger than the width and length of the tapestry.

3. Set aside the tapestry for now to create the lining. Fold the lining over 1" on the right and sew on the zipper. Work on one side of the zipper at a time.

4. Fold the lining on the other side over 1" and sew on the zipper. Both the zipper and the folds should be facing up.

5. Fold the lining in half with the zipper at the top and pin together. Sew two straight rows down both sides.

6. Hand sew the top of one side of the tapestry to the front of one side of the zipper.

7 Fold the tapestry in half around the lining and hand sew the other side of the tapestry to the other side of the zipper.

8 Tuck your lining inside the tapestry and hand sew up the sides of the tapestry. Use a strong, thin thread so that the sides butt up against each other and the warp selvedge is tightly sewn with the whip stitch.

9 Add a tassel to the zipper if you choose.

# Monogram Door Handle Decor

Add a subtle personal touch to your home without hanging a tapestry on the wall by creating some easy decor to hang on a door handle. This is an easy project and looks great with pom-poms or a tassel on the front. You can even sew it onto a fabric backing and fill it with potpourri to create an aromatic sachet.

For this project, you will need to find a hoop handle used for making bags, or a bangle bracelet. These are easy to find in the knitting, crochet, or jewelry sections of retail craft stores. Measure the section of it that will serve as the rod, so that you know how wide you want your tapestry.

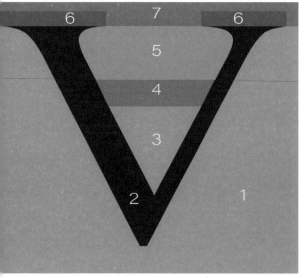

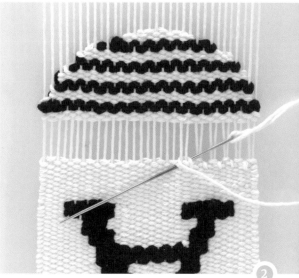

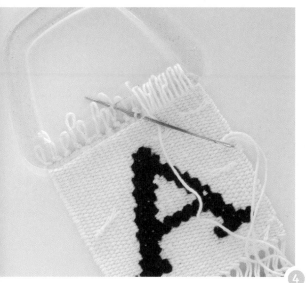

and the background at the same time, section by section. Start from the bottom (don't forget, you are weaving upside down!) and work upward. The letter *A*, for example, will have seven different sections, alternating between filling in the letter and the background.

③ Drape a piece of yarn from one side to the other of the bottom and use the larkshead knot to add fringe onto the drape.

④ When your tapestry is complete, attach it to the hoop handle, just as you would with a regular rod, and hang it on the doorknob.

① Print out your desired letter in large format. Use it as a template to trace the letter onto your warp, and fill it in.

② To keep your warp tension even while weaving detailed designs such as letters, work on filling in the template

# Diamond Twill Rug

Ready to take your skills to a large-scale project? You can use fabric strips to make a flatweave rug with any twill design! This project does require an extra-large loom, which you can easily make with a few 2-by-4 pieces of wood and a whole lot of nails.

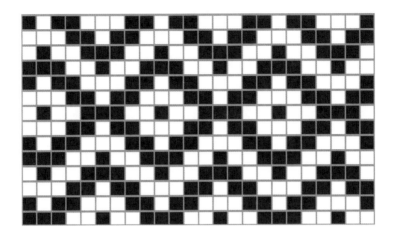

1. Prepare fabric strips for the warp and the weft (see page 141). Warp your loom the width of your rug. Make sure that all of your warp loops are even—if your loom has two rows of nails, warp only one of the rows.

2. Add a twining row to the very top and very bottom of your warp to keep the edges secure when you remove the rug from the loom.

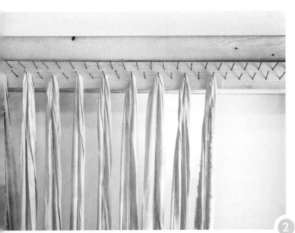

3. Add a strong dowel or rod the length of your warp, parallel to your warp on either edge. As you are weaving, treat the last warp string and the dowel as one. When you are working this large, with fabric, it is very easy for your sides to bow in, so the dowel will help anchor your edges and keep them straight. As with all weaving projects, don't forget to bubble your weft before beating it down!

4. If you notice that your sides are still bowing in a bit, even with the support from the dowel, you can tie the dowel to the frame of your loom to help pull it outward and straighten your edges.

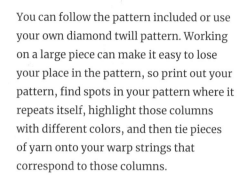

You can follow the pattern included or use your own diamond twill pattern. Working on a large piece can make it easy to lose your place in the pattern, so print out your pattern, find spots in your pattern where it repeats itself, highlight those columns with different colors, and then tie pieces of yarn onto your warp strings that correspond to those columns.

The last few rows will be extra tight, so unwrap your fabric from balls and use your fingers to guide it through. When you are finished weaving, tuck and trim any tails on the back. Then slide the dowels up out of each end of your rug and remove the warp from the loom.

Your rug is ready to use! Add a rubber backing below your rug to prevent it from slipping around and use it in a less trafficked area.

# Preparing Fabric Yarn

Create your own bundles of fabric scraps by easily knotting them together. If you want, you can dye the fabric a different color before cutting it.

1. Cut muslin into 2" strips. Cut 1" slits into both ends of your fabric strips. Guide a new strip of fabric through the slit of a previous strip.

2. Slip the tail of the new strip of fabric through its own slit.

3. Pull the strip through the slit until you reach the end.

4. Pull both strips to lock the knot in place.

5. Wrap connected strips into balls about 4" wide. If your ball of fabric strips gets too big it will be more difficult to guide it through the warp.

# Woven Patches

Add some personality to the holes in your clothing or home decor by weaving patches into any woven or knitted fabric. This technique works best if your fabric is thick, such as upholstery, denim, or wool sweaters, and the hole is not too large.

1. Turn your fabric inside out and stretch it on an embroidery hoop or frame, with the hole in the center. You will be weaving from the backside to add more durability.

2. Pick a few thin, durable yarn materials, such as upholstery thread, thread it onto a needle, and create a running stitch around the perimeter of the hole. This will help prevent your hole from continuing to fray.

3. Use the same thread to add warp strings across the back of the hole. Use the needle to help extend them above and below the hole into the fabric with running stitches. You can get creative with the shape of these stitches. If there is a section of fabric that is thin but hasn't frayed yet, extend the running stitches through it to add support.

4. Use thin, durable yarns to weave back and forth on the hole. They should loop around the short running stitches on either end. This is another part that you can get creative with by adding stripes or other design elements.

5. Complete weaving your design, packing the weft tightly and tucking all of your tails.

6. Turn the fabric inside out and trim any excess fraying so that it doesn't snag and pull the hole bigger.

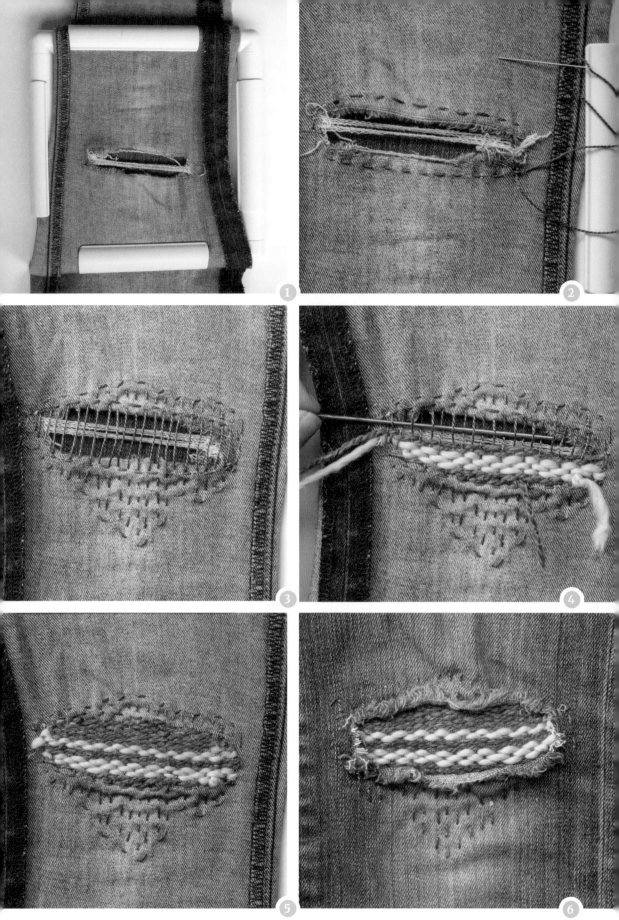

# Cross-Body Fringed Bag

A simple bit of sewing means you can make and wear your own cross-body bag. This is the perfect project to try out new techniques, such as pibione, and show them off!

1. Weave a piece of fabric that is 18" long by 8" wide, give or take, based on how big you want the finished piece. This will be folded in half to create the bag, so make sure the same design is reflected on either side. Knot the warp strings on both ends and trim them into short tassels to keep the design secure and to make sure they don't get in the way when you open the bag to reach inside.

2. Fold the woven piece in half so that the front sides are facing inward, and add zigzag stitches to the edges on top and bottom. If you don't have a sewing machine you can fold the woven piece in half so that the front sides are facing outward, and use a needle and thread to whipstitch the two sides together. You can also add a lining to the inside of the bag if you want to add durability (and if you know more about sewing).

3. Turn your bag inside out and poke out the corners.

4 Measure some rope or trim to go over your shoulder. Use a needle and yarn to tie the rope to the bag, about 3" to 4" from the top on either side, and knot the yarn on the inside. Leave an 8" tail of the rope below the yarn on either end.

5 Fold the tail of the rope back up, parallel to itself, and use a needle and yarn to securely wrap the two pieces together. Trim the tails.

6 If you want to add fringe to the bottom, cut lengths of about 10". Fold bundles of four to six in half and use a crochet needle to pull them through a row of weft at the bottom of the bag, securing them there with a larkshead knot.

7 The top of this bag is designed to flop over one side or the other for quick access as you're using it.

# Woven Vest and Other Clothing

Did you know that you can weave clothing? After all, weaving is a form of creating fabric! Weaving on a frame loom isn't as quick as on a rigid heddle loom, but it does allow you to add more details to your clothing piece and weave exactly the pattern that you need. Look for a pattern that doesn't have any pleats or darts, which can be more complex to weave. You can also make your own pattern by tracing a piece of clothing you have.

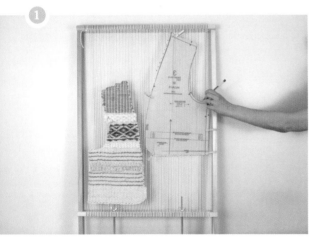

① Choose a sewing pattern for the woven clothing item you want to make. Look for sewing patterns that are marked as "easy" or "under one hour" with as few pieces as possible. The pattern I am using is McCalls 7276 Sewing Vest Pattern. Cut out your pattern, warp your loom, and trace the pattern straight onto your warp, using a heat- or water-soluble pen. Make sure the arrows on your pattern that mark the direction of the grain for your fabric are parallel to the warp on your loom.

2 Weave within the pattern you traced. You can add a twining row to bottom or top edges if you want. If there are parts of your clothing item that will visually flow from one piece to the next, make sure that the design in your weaving matches up on the seams. I used a repeating design to include a section of overshot in this vest. If you want, you can use this specific pattern and add it anywhere you wish. When all of your pattern pieces are woven you can cut them off the loom, leaving a 3" tail of warp extending from all appropriate edges.

3 Use a needle to tuck the warp through a few rows of weft, exiting out the backside of the piece and cutting off the tails.

4 When all of your weaving is finished and cut off the loom, and the warp strings are secured and backsides are clean, you will have the exact pieces you need!

5 Follow the sewing pattern's instructions and sew any seams together from the backside of the patterns.

6 Use a small zigzag stitch along all the edges of your project, even if there aren't any seams. This is an extra step to secure your warp strings within the fabric.

7 Add trim to the edges of the pattern if you want to smooth the appearance of any edges or protect them.

8 Now your piece is ready to be worn!

Looking for the perfect loom? Head to www.hellohydrangea.com for my unique design of looms that are adjustable WHILE you are weaving. Gamechangers for any project you are working on.

# RESOURCES

# Anatomy of a Loom

**A** Frame loom. A simple loom involving pegs/notches on polar ends of a frame to hold the vertical warp strings taut.

**B** Warp knotted on top. Begin and end your warp on the side of the loom farthest away from you.

**C** Sword. Also known as a pick-up stick or batten, this is used to lift half of the warp strings and open the shed.

**D** Heddle. Device used for faster weaving. Lifts the other half of the warp strings to open the warp shed, so that the shuttle can quickly pass through.

**E** Tapestry needle. A long, smooth needle with a large eye, used to tuck in tails and weave details.

**F** Warp. Strings held taut, vertically, across the loom.

**G** Shuttle. A tool that guides the weft through the shed.

**H** Felt tip marker. Used to draw outlines onto the warp.

**I** Warp shed. The space created between warp strings when some are lifted up for the shuttle to pass through to create rows of weft.

**J** Beater comb. A tool with teeth that is used to push rows of weft in place.

**K** Weft. Yarn guided through the shed to create horizontal rows.

**L** Low-density warp. Warp is more spread out, with fewer warp strings per inch. Used for looser, quicker weaving.

**M** High-density warp. Warp is closer together, with more warp strings per inch. Used for tighter, detailed weaving.

● Scissors (not shown).

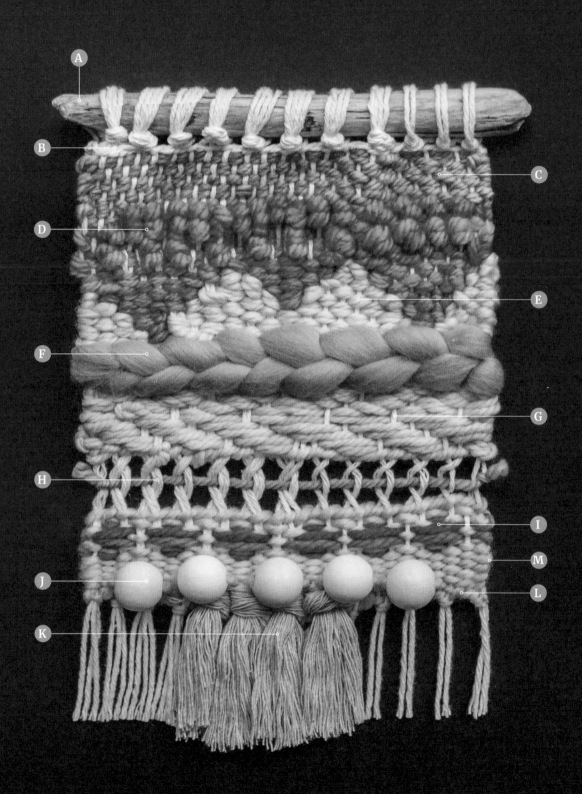

# Anatomy of a Tapestry

A Rod. A straight item to hang the tapestry from, usually 1–2" wider than the width of the tapestry.

B Twining header. The first row used to hold the following rows in place.

C Plain tabby weave. The basic plain weave; alternately goes over and under the warp strings.

D Pile weave. Loops created during tabby weave that extend beyond the surface of the tapestry.

E Shapes. Edges created from stairsteps as the weft rows pass over the warp strings.

F Soumak. A technique to create looped braiding effect.

G Twill. As rows of weft are added, the exposed warp strings create patterns.

H Leno. When a weft string holds manipulated warp strings in place.

I Supplementary weft. An additional weft that floats behind regular tabby rows and comes to the surface of the tapestry only to create patterns.

J Embellishments. Beads, tassels, baubles, and extra items that are added to the surface of the tapestry.

K Rya. A technique to create fringe and texture.

L Hem stitch. The last row used to hold the previous rows in place.

M Selvedge. The last few warp strings on either side of a tapestry.

# Glossary of Terms

**balanced weave:** Going over the same number of warp strings that you go under.

**beating:** Pressing a row of weft yarn into place with a beater device such as a comb.

**blanket stitch:** Used to attach fabric to a tapestry.

**blocking:** Post-weaving technique to fix puckering/bulging by using heat and steam.

**blocks:** Square or rectangle shapes.

**Brooks bouquet:** Weaving technique of wrapping bundles of warps together with a weft string.

**bubbling:** The act of creating hills of weft during tabby to maintain tension.

**bulging:** When a tapestry is cut off the loom and the warp strings expand apart due to improper tension, causing the edges or middle to curve outward.

**carpeted rya:** Weaving technique with rows of tightly packed rya, cut short.

**circle:** Shape with curved edges.

**concave selvedges:** Edges of a tapestry bow inward.

**convex selvedges:** Edges of a tapestry bow outward.

**double soumak:** Weaving technique of weaving two tails as soumak at once.

**dovetail:** Rows of weft overlap by a single warp string, alternating between short and long.

**draping:** Weaving technique letting yarn hang in an arch.

**draw in:** When the edges of the weave curve inward during weaving due to improper tension, such as the weft being too tight. See concave selvedges.

**Egyptian knot:** The soumak technique done backward.

**epi:** "Ends per inch" applies to the thickness of warp strings and how many will make up an inch when laid touching, side by side.

Low epi means thinner yarn; high epi means thicker yarn.

**fiber:** A material used to make yarn.

**flat weave:** Two-dimensional weaving technique to create patterns within the surface of the weave. The weft is guided back and forth through the warp continuously.

**float:** A warp or weft yarn that travels over more than one adjacent warp or weft.

**floating selvedge:** The last warp string on either side that can break the pattern to allow the weft to loop around the end.

**floating tabby:** Balanced weave of tabby that goes over and under more than one warp string at a time.

**free-form:** Weaving freely, not constrained by rows.

**full pass:** Two rows of balanced tabby weave.

**gaping:** When a straight split does not butt up together, creating a gap in the tapestry.

**ghiordes knot:** The most common rya technique.

**gradient:** Two or more colors fading into each other.

**half pass:** One row of balanced tabby weave.

**hanger:** The piece of string at the top of a rod to hang the tapestry on the wall.

**hatching:** Rows of weft overlap by many warp strings, alternating between short and long.

**heddle:** A device using fiber leashes to pick up a pattern of warp strings at the same time so that the shuttle can easily pass through the open shed.

**hem stitch:** A weaving technique to end tapestries; pulls warp strings together to hold the rows above in place.

**interlocking:** Rows of weft join at the turn to connect a straight split.

**joining:** Sewing up a straight split to avoid gaping.

keyhole tassel: A tassel that has a round head with a hole in the center and a straight skirt; resembles a keyhole.

knot and slip: A technique to attach a tapestry to a rod by slipping the rod through the warp loops.

krabbasnar: A weaving technique using a single supplementary warp to build vertical columns.

larkshead knot: Folding a length of yarn in half and slipping the tails through the loop around an item.

leno: A gauze-type weaving technique that twists warps together in an open weave.

loom: A tool used to hold warp strings taut during weaving.

loop and tail: A way to tie off the neck of a tassel without using any extra tools, by pulling both tails below the neck using an attached loop of the same yarn.

looped rya: Fringe that drapes between itself.

needle: A long, thin tool with an eye to guide the weft through the shed.

notches: Nails or guides on either side of a loom to hold the warp in place.

open shapes: Areas in a weave where the warp is left visible.

overshot: A supplementary weft technique where the extra weft floats behind the width of the tapestry when it is not used on the surface.

pencil roving: A thinner, slightly spun roving.

pibione: A weaving technique creating loops of pile weave in a pattern or shape.

pick and pick: Vertical stripes created from two different-colored tabby rows.

pick-up stick / shed stick: A tool used to open the shed for faster weaving.

pile weave: A weaving technique to create loops by wrapping tabby between warp strings onto a smooth rod, such as a knitting needle.

pom-pom: A bushy, textural ball of yarn where the tails face outward.

pulled thread: A weaving technique manipulating the warp strings with a row of weft and leaving the warp visible.

roving: An unspun material before the yarn stage.

rya: A weaving technique to create fringe.

sapma: A supplementary weft technique using two tails that cross within the shed.

selvedge: The edges of the tapestry, marked by the last warp yarns.

sett: Number of warp strings per inch.

shed: The open space created when the warp is separated to allow the weft to be guided through.

shot: One row of weft.

shuttle: Device to guide the weft through the warp; can be a needle or pick-up stick.

soumak: A weaving technique that wraps the weft around the warp in a braid-like effect.

Spanish lace: A weaving technique creating small shapes within a single row of weft.

straight split: The edges of two shapes that end on parallel warp strings and butt up but do not connect.

supplementary weft: A weaving technique using a foundational tabby weft as well as a floating weft to create patterns and shapes.

tabby/plain weave: The weft travels over and under the warp evenly without any floats. Can be weft dominant or warp dominant.

tails: End pieces of yarn.

tapestry weaving: Freestyle weaving done with your fingers.

tapestry/panel/weave/wall hanging: Finished product produced from combining weft and warp yarn on a frame loom.

tassel head: The top part of a tassel that looks like a knot and is the part that you attach to a tapestry.

tassel neck: The middle part of a tassel with material tied around the bundle of yarn to hold it in place.

**tassel skirt:** The bottom part of a tassel where the bundle of yarn is cut into fringe.

**template:** Using a predrawn design as reference for weaving.

**tension:** The push and pull of weft versus warp.

**triangle:** A shape with three sides.

**twill:** An unbalanced weaving technique where floating tabby rows create patterns.

**twining header:** Woven at the beginning of a tapestry to keep the warp evenly spaced to its full width and hold the following weaves in place.

**twisted floaters:** A weaving technique where the weft during a tabby row floats and twists.

**varied loops:** A weaving technique after a row of tabby to pull out bumps of the material between warp strings.

**warp:** The vertical strings in a tapestry, held taut on a loom during weaving.

**warp dominant:** When you see more warp because it is emphasized by the spacing of rows or thickness of material.

**warp string / warp thread:** A spun fiber material that is strong, durable, and smooth. Usually cotton.

**weave:** Technique in which warp and weft yarns intersect while being held taut on a loom to create a packed panel.

**weaver's knot:** The best method to securely combine two ends of yarn of the same color so that they are invisible among the weave.

**weft:** The horizontal strings in a tapestry, which move through the shed with tapestries and shuttles.

**weft dominant:** When you see more weft because it is emphasized by the spacing of rows or thickness of material.

**weft hooking:** When working with two wefts at once, a technique to hook them at the end of the row.

**wool top:** Roving.

**yarn/thread/string:** Materials used in weaving.

# Acknowledgments

The opportunity to write a second book has reminded me how thankful I am for the support I have been blessed with in my life. Thank you to my wonderful husband, Spencer Campbell, for cheering me on and pushing me to give all my best effort. Thank you to my friend Adria for stepping in and helping me manage my responsibilities as a mom during this whirlwind project. Thank you to my son, Clayton, for being the most patient two-year-old ever, and understanding that mama needs time to work with her "yarn." Thank you to my team at Schiffer for offering me the opportunity to round out my first book with a sequel and figuring out how to make it cohesive, yet able to stand on its own. I'm so happy that I was able to add another chapter to my love story with weaving! Thank you to all my mentors who have each taught me something that I needed to learn in the different chapters of my life.

hello hydrangea

*Lindsey Campbell* is the artist and instructor behind Hello Hydrangea. She has taught thousands of students how to weave through her online weaving video classes. Her work has been seen in Anthropologie, Nordstrom, Jo-Ann Fabric and Craft, *Koel* magazine, *In Her Studio* magazine, and Design*Sponge, and is numbered among the 10 Best Craft Blogs by My Modern Met. Lindsey lives in California with her husband, son, and their miniature schnauzer. You can find her at www.hellohydrangea.com.